TABLE OF CONTENTS

HOW TO USE THIS BOOK

Your *Fish of Arizona Field Guide* is designed to make it easy to identify more than 75 species of the most common and important fish in Arizona, and learn fascinating facts about each species' range, natural history and more.

The fish are organized by families, such as Catfish (*Ictaluridae*), Perch (*Percidae*), Trout and Salmon (*Salmonidae*) and Sunfish (*Centrarchidae*), which are listed in alphabetical order. Within these families, individual species are arranged alphabetically in their appropriate groups. For example, members of the Sunfish family are divided into Black Bass, Crappie and True Sunfish groups. For a detailed list of fish families and individual species, turn to the Table of Contents (page 3); the Index (pp. 170-173) provides a handy reference guide to fish by common name (such as Brown Trout) and other common terms for the species.

Fish Identification

Determining a fish's body shape is the first step to identifying it. Each fish family usually exhibits one or sometimes two basic outlines. Catfish have long, stout bodies with flattened heads, barbels or "whiskers" around the mouth, a relatively tall but narrow dorsal fin and an adipose fin. There are two forms of Sunfish: the flat, round, plate-like outline we see in Bluegills; and the torpedo or "fusiform" shape of Largemouth Bass.

In this field guide you can quickly identify a fish by first matching its general body shape to one of the fish family silhouettes listed in the Table of Contents. From there, turn to that family's section and use the illustrations and text descriptions to identify your fish. A Sample Page (pg. 22) is provided to explain how the information is presented in each two-page spread.

For some species, the illustration will be enough to identify your catch, but it is important to note that your fish may not look exactly like the artwork. Fish frequently change colors. Males that are brightly colored during the spawning season may show muted coloration at other times. Likewise, bass caught in muddy streams show much less pattern than those taken from clear lakes—and all fish lose some of their markings and color when removed from the water.

Most fish are similar in appearance to one or more other species—often, but not always, within the same family. For example, the Black Crappie is remarkably similar to the White Crappie. To accurately identify such look-alikes, check the inset illustrations and accompanying notes below the main illustration, under the "Similar Species" heading.

Throughout *Fish of Arizona* we use basic biological and fisheries management terms that refer to physical characteristics or conditions of fish and their environment, such as "*dorsal*" fin or "*turbid*" water. For your convenience, these are listed and defined in the Glossary (pp. 164-168), along with other handy fish-related terms and their definitions.

Understanding such terminology will help you make sense of reports on state and federal research, fish population surveys, lake assessments, management plans and other important fisheries documents.

FISH ANATOMY

It's much easier to identify fish if you know the names of different parts of a fish. For example, it's easier to use the term "adipose" fin to indicate the small, soft, fleshy flap on an Apache Trout's back than try to describe it. The following illustrations point out the basic parts of a fish; the accompanying text defines these characteristics.

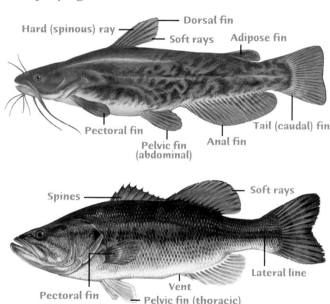

Fins are made up of bony structures that support a membrane. There are three kinds of bony structures in fins: **Soft rays** are flexible fin supports and are often branched.

Spines are stiff, often sharp supports that are not jointed. **Hard rays** are stiff, pointed, barbed structures that can be raised or lowered. Catfish are famous for their hard rays, which are often mistakenly called spines. Sunfish have soft rays associated with spines to form a prominent dorsal fin.

Fins are named by their position on the fish. The **dorsal fin** is on top along the midline. A few species have another fin on their back, called an **adipose fin**. This small, fleshy protuberance located between the dorsal fin and the tail is distinctive of catfish, trout and salmon. **Pectoral fins** are found on each side of the fish near the gills. The **anal fin** is located along the midline, on the fish's bottom or *ventral* side. There is also a paired set of fins on the bottom of the fish, called the **pelvic fins**. These can be in the **thoracic position** (just below the pectoral fins) or farther back on the stomach, in the **abdominal position**. The tail is known as the **caudal fin**.

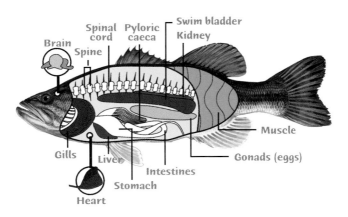

Eyes—A fish's eyes can detect color. Their eyes are rounder than those of mammals because of the refractive index of water; focus is achieved by moving the lens in and out, not distorting it as in mammals. Different species have varying levels of eyesight. Walleyes see well in low light. Bluegills have excellent daytime vision but see poorly at night, making them vulnerable to predation.

Nostrils—A pair of nostrils, or *nares*, are used to detect odors in the water. Eels and catfishes have particularly well-developed senses of smell.

Mouth—The shape of the mouth is a clue to what the fish eats. The larger the food it consumes, the larger the mouth.

Teeth—Not all fish have teeth, but those that do have mouthgear designed to help them feed. Walleyes, Northern Pike and Tiger Muskies have sharp *canine* teeth for grabbing and holding prey. Minnows have *pharyngeal* teeth—located in the throat—for grinding.

Catfish have *cardiform* teeth, which feel like a rough patch in the front of the mouth. Bass have patches of *vomerine* teeth on the roof of their mouth.

Swim Bladder—Almost all fish have a swim bladder, a balloon-like organ that helps the fish regulate its buoyancy.

Lateral Line—This sensory organ helps the fish detect movement in the water (to help avoid predators or capture prey) as well as water currents and pressure changes. It consists of fluid filled sacs with hair-like sensors, which are open to the water through a row of pores in their skin along each side—creating a visible line along the fish's side.

FISH NAMES

A Walleye is a Walleye in Arizona. But in the northern parts of its range, Canadians call it a jack or jackfish. In the eastern U.S. it is often called a pickerel or walleyed pike.

Because common names may vary regionally, and even change for different sizes of the same species, scientific names are used that are exactly the same around the world. Each species has only one correct scientific name that can be recognized anywhere, in any language. The Walleye is *Sander vitreus* from Tucson to Tokyo.

Scientific names are made up of Greek or Latin words that often describe the species. There are two parts to a scientific name: the generic or "genus," which is capitalized (*Sander*), and the specific name, which is not capitalized (*vitreus*). Both are displayed in italic text.

A species' genus represents a group of closely related fish. The Walleye and Sauger are in the same genus, so they share the generic name *Sander*. But each have different specific names, *vitreus* for Walleye, *canadense* for the Sauger.

ABOUT ARIZONA FISH

In spite of being a desert state, Arizona is rich in aquatic diversity. Habitats range from gin-clear, high-elevation streams and lakes to the mighty Colorado River and tiny desert springs. As a result, Arizona offers a profusion of opportunities to watch, study and pursue fish. This guide covers the 27 species commonly pursued by anglers, along with most native and introduced nongame species.

12

FREQUENTLY ASKED QUESTIONS

What is a fish?

Fish are aquatic, typically cold-blooded animals that have backbones, gills and fins.

Are all fish cold-blooded?

All freshwater fish are cold-blooded. Recently it has been discovered that some members of the saltwater Tuna family are warm-blooded. Whales and Bottlenose Dolphins are also warm-blooded, but they are mammals, not fish.

Do all fish have scales?

No. Most fish have scales that look like those on the Common Goldfish. A few, such as Alligator Gar, have scales that resemble armor plates. Catfish have no scales at all.

How do fish breathe?

A fish takes in water through its mouth and forces it through its gills, where a system of fine membranes absorbs oxygen from the water, and releases carbon dioxide. Gills cannot pump air efficiently over these membranes, which quickly dry out and stick together. Fish should never be out of the water longer than you can hold your breath.

Can fish breathe air?

Some species can; gars have a modified swim bladder that acts like a lung. Fish that can't breathe air may die when dissolved oxygen in the water falls below critical levels.

How do fish swim?

Fish swim by contracting bands of muscles on alternate sides of their body so the tail is whipped rapidly from side to side. Pectoral and pelvic fins are used mainly for stability when a fish hovers, but are sometimes used during rapid bursts of forward motion.

Do all fish look like fish?

Most do and are easily recognizable as fish. The eels and lampreys are fish, but they look like snakes. Sculpins look like little goblins with bat wings.

Where can you find fish?

Some fish species can be found in almost any body of water, but not all fish are found everywhere. Each is designed to exploit a particular habitat. The Gila Chub is found in small headwater streams, springs and marshes, while the Colorado Pikeminnow prefers large rivers.

A species may move around within its home water, sometimes migrating hundreds of miles between lakes, rivers and tributary streams. Some movements, such as spawning migrations, are seasonal and very predictable.

Fish may also move horizontally from one area to another, or vertically in the water column, in response to changes in environmental conditions and food availability. In addition, many fish have daily travel patterns. By studying a species' habitat, food and spawning information in this book—and understanding how it interacts with other Arizona fish—it is possible to make an educated prediction of where to find it in any lake, stream or river.

WHIRLING DISEASE

Whirling disease affects trout and salmon. It is thought to be a major factor in the decline of wild Rainbow Trout in some Western waters. It is caused by a microscopic parasite (*Myxobolus cerebralis*) that attacks soft cartilage, causing nerve damage, skeletal deformities and sometimes death. The disease likely originated in Europe, where native Brown Trout are resistant to the parasite.

Whirling disease has been confirmed in Lee's Ferry, but the Arizona Game and Fish Department is working hard to help control and prevent its spread.

You Can Help
- Wash off any mud from vehicles, boats, trailers, anchors, axles, waders, boots, fishing equipment and anything that can hold the spores or mud-dwelling worms.

- Drain boats, coolers, bait wells and any holder of water.

- Don't transport fish from one body of water to another. It is unlawful in Arizona to move live fish without a license.

- Don't dispose of fish entrails in any body of water.

- Never transport aquatic plants. Make sure boats, props, anchors and trailers are cleared of weeds after every use.

INVASIVE SPECIES

While many introduced species have great recreational value, such as Largemouth Bass, many exotic species have caused problems. Never move fish, water or vegetation from one lake or stream to another. For details, visit the Game and Fish website, www.azgfd.gov.

FUN WITH FISH

There are many ways to enjoy Arizona's fish, from reading about them in this book to watching them in the wild. You can don a dive mask and jump in, wear polarized glasses to observe them from above the surface, or use an underwater camera (or sonar) to monitor fish behavior year-round.

Hands-on activities are also popular. More than 400,000 residents and nonresidents enjoy fishing for Arizona's game fish. The sport offers a great chance to enjoy the outdoors with friends and family, and in many cases, bring home a healthy meal of fresh fish at the end of the day.

Proceeds from license sales, along with special taxes anglers pay on fishing supplies and motorboat fuel, fund the majority of fish management efforts, including fish surveys, the development of special regulations and stocking programs. The sport also has more than a $1 billion impact on Arizona's economy, supporting thousands of jobs in fishing, tourism and related industries.

If you would like to learn how to fish, Arizona's Sport Fishing Educational Program can help you become more proficient in basic fishing techniques. The program is conducted in a safe, friendly learning environment and is designed for beginning anglers. This statewide program is designed to take advantage of the many fishable waters available in both rural and urban areas. The Game and Fish Department supplies all educational materials, rods, reels, bait and instruction. Normal fishing license requirements are waived during a department-sponsored fishing program. All fishing programs are offered free of charge.

OPPORTUNITIES FOR NONRESIDENTS

Nearly 70,000 nonresidents sample Arizona's remarkable fisheries each year. A wealth of resources are available to help out-of-state anglers (as well as residents) enjoy the full bounty of opportunities.

One source is the Game and Fish website: www.azgfd.gov.

Here you'll find lots of helpful information, including stocking schedules, fishing reports, updates on water conditions and fish populations, and more.

Information is also available at the following numbers:

Pinetop Region: (928) 367-4281

Flagstaff Region: (928) 774-5045

Kingman Region: (928) 692-7700

Yuma Region: (928) 342-4051

Tucson Region: (520) 388-4451

Mesa Region: (480) 324-3544

In addition, outfitters, guides, fly shops and bait dealers are great resources. So are reputable fishing organizations such as the Arizona Anglers Family Fishing Club (www.azod.org/aaff), Southwest Walleye Anglers (www.swwalleye.com) and local chapters of Trout Unlimited (www.tu.org).

CATCH-AND-RELEASE FISHING

Selective harvest (keeping some fish to eat and releasing the rest) and total catch-and-release fishing allow anglers to enjoy the sport without harming the resource. Catch-and-release is especially important with certain species and sizes of fish, and in lakes or rivers where biologists are trying to improve the fishery by protecting large predators or breeding age, adult fish. The fishing regulations, Game and Fish website and your local fisheries office are excellent sources of advice on which fish to keep or release.

Catch-and-release is only truly successful if the fish survives the experience. Following are helpful tips to help reduce the chances of post-release mortality.

- Play and land fish quickly.

- Wet your hands before touching a fish, to avoid removing its protective slime coating.

- Handle the fish gently and keep it in the water if possible.

- Do not hold the fish by the eye sockets or gills. Hold it horizontally and support its belly.

- If a fish is deeply hooked, cut the line so at least an inch hangs outside the mouth. This helps the hook lie flush when the fish takes in food.

- Circle hooks may help reduce deeply hooked fish.

- Don't fish deep water unless you plan to keep your catch.

- Don't release fish kept on a stringer or in a livewell. In Arizona, these fish count in your limit.

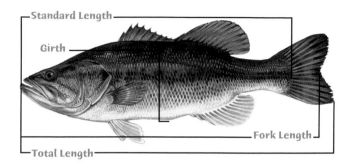

FISH MEASUREMENT

Fish are measured in three ways: standard length, fork length and total length. The first two are more accurate, because tails are often damaged or worn down. Total length is used in slot limits.

The following formulas estimate the weight of popular game fish. Lengths are in inches; weight is in pounds.

Formulas

Bass weight = (length x length x girth) / 1,200
Pike weight = (length x length x length) / 3,500
Sunfish weight = (length x length x length) / 1,200
Trout weight = (length x girth x girth) / 800
Walleye weight = (length x length x length) / 2,700

For example, let's say that you catch a 16-inch Walleye. Using the formula for Walleyes above: (16 x 16 x 16) divided by 2,700 = 1.5 pounds. Your Walleye would weigh approximately 1.5 pounds.

ARIZONA STATE RECORD FISH

SPECIES	WEIGHT (LBS.-0Z.)	WHERE CAUGHT	YEAR
Bass, Largemouth	16-7.68	Canyon Lake	1997
Bass, Rock	0-12.96	Upper Verde River	2006
Bass, Smallmouth	7-0.96	Roosevelt Lake	1988
Bass, Striped	27-4.48	Lake Pleasant	2007
Bass, White	4-11.7	Upper Lake Pleasant	1972
Bass, Yellow	1-15.8	Upper Lake Mary	1995
Bluegill	3-15.68	Goldwater Lake	2004
Buffalo, Bigmouth	36-6	Roosevelt Lake	1995
Buffalo, Black	35-6.72	Canyon Lake	1995
Bullhead, Black	2-6.1	Parker Canyon Lake	2002
Bullhead, Yellow	4-8.1	Mormon Lake	1989
Carp	37-0	Bartlett Lake	1987
Catfish, Channel	32-4	Parker Canyon Lake	1987
Catfish, Flathead	71-10.24	San Carlos Lake	2003
Crappie, Black	4-10	San Carlos Lake	1959
Crappie, White	3-5.28	Lake Pleasant	1982
Grayling, Arctic	1-9.76	Lee Valley Lake	1995
Mullet	5-2.24	Fortuna Pond	2004
Northern Pike	32-5.6	Ashurst Lake	2004
Roundtail Chub*	3-14.9	Lower Salt River	1984
Sucker, Desert**	2-10.75	Verde River	1992
Sucker, Sonora	5-6.4	Canal Park Lake	1996
Sunfish, Green	1-9	Parker Canyon Lake	1996
Sunfish, Hybrid*	2-2.22	Patagonia Lake	1998
Sunfish, Redear	3-9	Goldwater Lake	1993
Tilapia	7-8.8	Saguaro Lake	2002
Trout, Apache**	5-15.5	Hurricane Lake***	1993
Trout, Brook	4-15.2	Sunrise Lake***	1995
Trout, Brown	22-14.5	Reservation Lake***	1999
Trout, Cutthroat	6-5	Luna Lake	1976
Trout, Rainbow	15-9.12	Willow Springs Lake	2006
Walleye	16-1.76	Show Low Lake	2002
White Amur	47-1.6	Encanto Park Lake	2002
Yellow Perch	1-10	Stoneman Lake	1984

Colorado River Waters: Hook and Line

Bass, Largemouth	16-14	Colorado River	1996
Bass, Smallmouth	5-2.72	Colorado River	1997
Bass, Striped**	67-1	Colorado River	1997
Bass, White	5-5	Imperial Reservoir	1972
Bluegill	2-11.5	Lake Mead	1989
Bullhead, Yellow	2-8.8	Colorado River	1986

SPECIES	WEIGHT (LBS.-0Z.)	WHERE CAUGHT	YEAR
Carp	42-0	Lake Havasu	1979
Catfish, Channel	35-4	Topock Marsh	1952
Catfish, Flathead	74-0	Colorado River	1998
Crappie, Black	2-12	Lake Havasu	1996
Mullet	9-8	Col./Gila confluence	1976
Pacific Tenpounder	0-12.6	near Pilot Knob	1981
Sucker, Razorback*p	9-13	Lake Havasu	1978
Sunfish, Green	1-5.28	Lake Havasu	1997
Sunfish, Hybrid*	3-1.28	Colorado River	2000
Sunfish, Redear	3-9.6	Lake Havasu	2005
Tilapia	6-2.72	Colorado River	2006
Trout, Brook	5-4	Lee's Ferry	1982
Trout, Brown	17-0	Last Chance Bay, Powell	1971
Trout, Cutthroat	9-8	S. of Davis Dam	1979
Trout, Rainbow	21-5.5	Willow Beach	1966
Walleye	8-1	Lake Powell	1977
Warmouth	0-12	Senator Lake	1974

* Larger than current "All Tackle" world record listed by the National Fresh Water Fishing Hall of Fame.
** World record for "All Tackle" as verified by the National Fresh Water Fishing Hall of Fame.
*** Fort Apache Indian Reservation.
p Species now protected, may not be taken.

FISH CONSUMPTION ADVISORIES

Most fish are safe for us to eat. They are also a healthy source of low-fat protein. But because most of the world's surface water contains some industrial contaminants, and Arizona's lakes and rivers are no exception, any store-bought or sport-caught fish could contain mercury, PCBs or other contaminants.

The state offers information on eating sport-caught species. Visit www.azgfd.gov/h_f/fish_consumption.shtml for details, or download the Department of Environmental Quality's fact sheet at http://www.azdeq.gov/environ/water/assessment/download/fish0305.pdf.

Description: brief summary of physical characteristics to help you identify the fish, such as coloration and markings, body shape, fin size and placement

Similar Species: list of other fish that look similar and the pages on which they can be found; includes detailed inset drawings (below) highlighting key physical traits such as markings, mouth size or shape and fin characteristics to help you distinguish this fish from similar species

Rainbow Trout	Brook Trout	Rainbow Trout	Brown Trout
lacks worm-like markings	worm-like marks on back	pinkish stripe on silvery body	sides lack pinkish stripe

COMMON NAME

Scientific Name

Other Names: common terms or nicknames you may hear to describe this species

Habitat: environment where the fish is found (such as streams, rivers, small or large lakes, fast-flowing or still water, in or around vegetation, near shore, in clear water)

Range: geographic distribution, starting with the fish's overall range, followed by state-specific information

Food: what the fish eats most of the time (such as crustaceans, insects, fish, plankton)

Reproduction: timing of and behavior during the spawning period (such as dates and water temperatures, migration information, preferred spawning habitat, type of nest if applicable, colonial or solitary nester, parental care for eggs or fry)

Average Size: average length or range of length, average weight or range of weight

Records: state—the state record for this species, location and year; North American—the North American record for this species, location and year (from the National Fresh Water Fishing Hall of Fame)

Notes: interesting natural history information; this can be unique behaviors, remarkable features, sporting and table quality, or details on annual migrations, seasonal patterns or population trends

Description: back black to olive; sides yellowish green; belly cream to yellow; light bar on base of tail; barbels (dark at base) around mouth; adipose fin; scaleless skin; rounded tail

Similar Species: Yellow Bullhead (pg. 26), Flathead Catfish (pg. 30)

Black Bullhead	**Yellow Bullhead**	**Black Bullhead**	**Flathead Catfish**
usually 15 to 21 anal fin rays	usually 24 to 27 anal fin rays	slight overbite	pronounced underbite

Black Bullhead	**Yellow Bullhead**
olive back and sides	yellowish back and sides

BLACK BULLHEAD

Ameiurus melas

Ictaluridae

Other Names: mud cat, common bullhead, horned pout

Habitat: shallow, slow-moving streams and backwaters; lakes and ponds—tolerates extremely turbid (cloudy) conditions; prefers silt bottom and lack of noticeable current

Range: southern Canada through the Great Lakes and the Mississippi River watershed into Mexico and the Southwest; reported in waters across Arizona, but does best in murky-water systems with few other fish

Food: a scavenging opportunist, feeds mostly on animal material (live or dead) but will eat plant matter

Reproduction: spawns in spring into early summer; excavates nest in shallow water with a muddy bottom; both sexes guard nest and eggs, which hatch in 4 to 6 days; adults guard young until they are about 1 inch in length; fry school in tight swarms along shorelines through their first summer

Average Size: 8 to 10 inches; 4 ounces to 1 pound

Records: state—2 pounds, 6.1 ounces, Parker Canyon Lake, 2002; North American—8 pounds, 15 ounces, Sturgis Pond, Michigan, 1987

Notes: The Black Bullhead arrived in Arizona in 1920. It is easy to catch and its white fillets have a good flavor, though they can become soft in summer. It tolerates silt, pollution, low oxygen levels and warm water. Adults typically rest in deep water by day, then move shallower as darkness falls to scavenge until shortly before daybreak.

Description: olive head and back; yellowish-green sides; white belly. Barbells on lower jaw are pale green to white; scaleless skin; adipose fin, rounded tail

Similar Species: Black Bullhead (pg. 24), Flathead Catfish (pg. 30)

Yellow Bullhead	**Black Bullhead**	**Yellow Bullhead**	**Flathead Catfish**
usually 24 to 27 anal fin rays	usually 15 to 21 anal fin rays	slight overbite	pronounced underbite

Yellow Bullhead	**Black Bullhead**
yellowish back and sides	olive back and sides

YELLOW BULLHEAD

Ameiurus natalis

Other Names: white-whiskered bullhead, yellow cat

Habitat: medium-size streams and shallows of warmwater lakes; prefers clear water and rocky bottom

Range: southern Great Lakes through eastern U.S. to the Gulf and into Mexico, introduced in the West; widespread in Arizona, including lower Colorado, Salt and Verde rivers, and Apache, Mormon, Parker Canyon and Roper lakes

Food: a scavenging opportunist that feeds mainly at night on aquatic insects, crayfish, snails, small fish and plant matter

Reproduction: in early summer female and male build nest in shallow water with a sand or rocky bottom, often in cover offering shade; both sexes guard eggs and young

Average Size: 7 to 13 inches, 4 to 19 ounces

Records: state—4 pounds, 8.1 ounces, Mormon Lake, 1989; North American—4 pounds, 15 ounces, Ogeechie River, Georgia, 2003

Notes: Uses its acute sense of smell to locate food and in social behavior. Although it is found in streams with permanent flow, it tends to avoid strong currents. Not widely pursued by anglers but its cream-colored flesh has an excellent flavor, though it may become soft during the summer months. Easily caught by fishing worms or crickets on the bottom at night. More carnivorous than the Black Bullhead.

Description: gray to silver back and sides; white belly; black spots on sides; large fish lack spots and appear dark olive or slate; forked tail; adipose fin; long barbels around mouth

Similar Species: Blue Catfish, Bullheads (pp. 24-26), Flathead Catfish (pg. 30)

Channel Catfish

deeply forked tail

Flathead Catfish

squared tail

Bullheads

tail rounded or slightly notched

Channel Catfish

anal fin curved, with 24 to 29 rays

Blue Catfish

anal fin straight, with 30 or more rays

CHANNEL CATFISH

Ictalurus punctatus

Other Names: spotted, speckled or silver catfish, fiddler

Habitat: prefers clean streams with moderate current, deep pools and sand, gravel or rubble bottom; stocked in many lakes; can tolerate turbid (cloudy) backwaters

Range: southern Canada through Midwest into Mexico and Florida; introduced through much of the U.S.; widespread in Arizona, found in most warmwater lakes and rivers

Food: insects, crustaceans, fish, some plant matter

Reproduction: typically matures at 3 to 6 years; spawns April through early June at water temperatures of 70 to 85 degrees F; male builds nest in dark, sheltered area such as undercut bank; female deposits 2,000 to 21,000 eggs, which hatch in 6 to 10 days; male guards eggs and young

Average Size: 12 to 20 inches, 3 to 4 pounds

Records: state—32 pounds, 4 ounces, Parker Canyon Lake, 1987; North American—58 pounds, Santee Cooper Reservoir, South Carolina, 1964

Notes: Introduced to Arizona in 1903, the Channel Catfish is a strong fighter caught on a variety of prepared baits. Its white, sweet fillets are excellent table fare. Often holds in deep water or cover during the day, then moves into riffles or other shallow areas at night. Primarily uses taste buds in its barbels and skin to locate food. However, its relatively large eyes also allow it to feed by sight. Typically a bottom feeder, it will suspend or rise to the surface on occasion.

Description: color variable, usually mottled yellow or brown; belly cream to yellow; adipose fin; chin barbels; lacks scales; head broad and flat; tail squared; pronounced underbite

Similar Species: Bullheads (pp. 24-26), Channel Catfish (pg. 28)

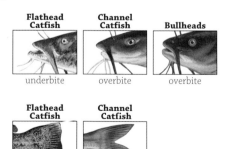

Flathead Catfish	Channel Catfish	Bullheads
underbite	overbite	overbite

Flathead Catfish	Channel Catfish
square tail	forked tail

FLATHEAD CATFISH

Pylodictis olivaris

Other Names: shovel-nose, shovelhead, yellow cat, mud cat, pied cat, Mississippi cat

Habitat: deep pools of large rivers and impoundments; often found near cover and in fast water below dams

Range: the Mississippi River watershed and into Mexico; large rivers in the Southwest; in Arizona, found in the lower Colorado River near Yuma, the Gila and Salt rivers, and the Verde River system and reservoirs

Food: fish, crayfish

Reproduction: matures at about 18 inches in length; spawns spring and early summer when water is 72 to 80 degrees F; male builds and defends nest in hollow log, undercut bank or other secluded area; female may lay more than 30,000 eggs; male guards young to about 7 days after hatching

Average Size: 15 to 45 inches; 1 to 45 pounds

Records: state—71 pounds, 10.24 ounces, San Carlos Lake, 2003; North American—123 pounds; Elk River Reservoir, Kansas, 1998

Notes: A large, typically solitary predator introduced to Arizona in the 1940s. A strong fighter with firm, white flesh. Feeds aggressively on live fish, often at night, when it moves from deep water in pools (or cover such as a logjam) to riffles and shallow areas of pools. It is not a scavenger and rarely eats decaying animal matter. In some waters it is blamed for reducing native fish populations.

Description: dark gray to black back with gray to white sides and belly; reddish coloration on fins, tail and under head; barbels black except on chin, where they appear white to gray; moderately forked tail

Similar Species: Channel Catfish (pg. 28)

Yaqui Catfish

Channel Catfish

dark body, short pectoral and dorsal spines

lighter coloration, longer spines

YAQUI CATFISH
Ictalurus pricei

Other Names: Price's Catfish

Habitat: ponds, streams and large rivers; prefers clear, quiet pools in streams, and sand or rocky substrate in moderate to slack current areas of rivers

Range: Rio Yaqui system in Chihuahua and Sonora, Mexico, and extreme southeast Arizona; reintroduced to San Bernardino National Wildlife Refuge

Food: fish, insects, crustaceans, plant matter

Reproduction: spawns in late spring; eggs are deposited in nest on bottom; male defends nest, incubates the eggs by fanning away silt, and guards the fry, which school in small swarms

Average Size: up to 22 inches

Records: none

Notes: Exceedingly rare, the Yaqui Catfish is Arizona's only native catfish and the only known member of the catfish family native to the Pacific Slope. During periods of low flows during the dry season, it will congregate in spring-fed pools. Though it is a tenacious desert dweller, it is vulnerable to predation and competition from non-native fish, as well as habitat destruction due to livestock grazing, groundwater pumping, water diversion and drought.

PACU

PIRANHA

Description: varied coloration, but often dark gray to silver or greenish-bronze; fine scales; large, deep body; large, round eye; small mouth; blunt teeth for crushing food items

Similar Species: Piranha

Pacu	Piranha
squarish, blunt teeth, slight underbite to overbite	sharp, pointed teeth, pronounced underbite

PACU

Colossoma or Piaractus sp.

Other Names: tambaqui, black pacu, pla paku, pirapitinga

Habitat: in its native range it is found in flooded rainforests of the Amazon basin

Range: native to the Amazon, Orinoco and La Plata river basins of South America; widely introduced due to aquarium releases or escapes from aquaculture facilities

Food: plant and animal matter

Reproduction: little is known of natural reproduction; believed to make spawning migrations to shoal areas

Average Size: some varieties reach weights of 20 to 60 pounds, but most individuals reported in Arizona are much smaller

Records: state—none; North American—11 pounds, 11 ounces, DeKalb Lake, Alabama, 1998

Notes: There are several varieties of Pacu, all of which are non-native. A popular aquarium fish, the Pacu is sometimes released into state waters and commonly mistaken for the Piranha. Arizona fisheries offices receive requests to identify these fish each year. In fact, the Pacu was included in this book at the request of the Game and Fish Department. An omnivore, it eats a variety of foods ranging from fruits and nuts to animal matter.

Description: olive-green back fading to silvery-white or pale, brassy sides and belly; adipose fin; blunt snout; black stripe through center of deeply forked tail

Similar Species: Threadfin Shad (pg. 42)

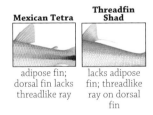

Mexican Tetra

adipose fin; dorsal fin lacks threadlike ray

Threadfin Shad

lacks adipose fin; threadlike ray on dorsal fin

MEXICAN TETRA
Astyanax mexicanus

Other Names: sardinita mexicana

Habitat: tolerates a variety of habitats, including rivers, wetlands, springs, canals and backwaters; prefers clear, shallow, flowing water and gravel bottom; seldom found in deep or weedy water

Range: subtropical America including the lower Rio Grande and Pecos rivers in Texas and New Mexico; introduced elsewhere; in Arizona, introduced in the Colorado River system

Food: fish, aquatic and terrestrial insects, snails, crayfish, filamentous algae and other plant matter

Reproduction: fish hatched in spring mature by first autumn; spawns year-round in suitable tropical habitat, late spring to early summer in cooler northern waters; adhesive eggs hatch in 24 hours

Average Size: up to 4¾ inches

Records: none

Notes: The Mexican Tetra belongs to a large family of about 800 fish species found mostly in Central and South America and Africa. It is closely related to the minnow family but distinguishable by its adipose fin and toothy jaws. May form dense schools that blacken the water. Most introductions are believed to be the results of bait-bucket releases. Makes an excellent aquarium fish.

MOZAMBIQUE
TILAPIA

CONVICT CICHLID

Description: variable coloration from gray, silver-gray and dark olive to metallic blue and yellowish; deep body similar to Bluegill; unbroken dorsal and anal fin with pointed ends

Similar Species: Black Crappie (pg. 142), Bluegill (pg. 146), Convict Cichlid

Tilapia	Bluegill	Black Crappie
two-part lateral line, front higher than rear	single lateral line	single lateral line

Tilapia	Convict Cichlid
three or four anal spines	five anal spines

TILAPIA
Oreochromis

Other Names: Mozambique mouthbrooder, Java Tilapia, largemouth kurper, Israeli Tilapia

Habitat: a variety of fresh and brackish water habitats; some species of Tilapia cannot tolerate temperatures below 50 degrees F

Range: native to tropical and subtropical Africa and the Middle East; widely introduced in North America, established in at least seven states including Arizona; areas within Arizona include the lower Colorado, Gila and Salt rivers; Alamo, Pleasant and Roper lakes; and canals and ditches between Phoenix and Yuma

Food: aquatic vegetation, algae

Reproduction: male guards territory and nest; female enters nest, deposits eggs and picks them up with her mouth; female retains fertilized eggs in mouth until hatching, typically in 10 to 12 days

Average Size: 4 to 18 inches, 6 ounces to 5 pounds

Records: state—7 pounds, 8.8 ounces, Saguaro Lake, 2002; North American—9 pounds, Big Lake Toho, Florida, 2003

Notes: At least four different species of Tilapia have been introduced to Arizona since the 1960s. Hybridization makes identification difficult. Often stocked for algae or weed control, but will take worms, crickets or doughballs. Mild-flavored fillets have excellent table qualities. Related to and often confused with non-native Convict Cichlid.

Description: silvery-blue back with white sides and belly; small mouth; last rays of dorsal fin form a long thread; deep body; young fish have a dark spot behind the gill flap

Similar Species: Threadfin Shad (pg. 42)

Gizzard Shad

Threadfin Shad

lower jaw does not project past tip of snout

lower jaw projects past tip of snout

Gizzard Shad

Threadfin Shad

no yellow on tail

yellow tail

GIZZARD SHAD

Dorosoma cepedianum

Other Names: hickory, mud or jack shad, skipjack

Habitat: quiet water of large rivers, reservoirs, lakes, swamps; brackish and saline waters in coastal areas

Range: St. Lawrence River and Great Lakes, Mississippi, Atlantic and Gulf Slope drainages from Quebec to Mexico, south into Florida, introduced elsewhere; in Arizona, it is established in Lake Powell and documented in Roosevelt

Food: plankton, algae, insects and other organic matter

Reproduction: spawns May through June in tributary streams and sheltered bays; mixed schools of males and females roil at the surface, releasing eggs and milt without regard for individual mates; adhesive eggs sink to bottom and hatch in 2 to 7 days

Average Size: 6 to 14 inches, 1 to 16 ounces

Records: state---none; North American—4 pounds, 12 ounces, Lake Oahe, South Dakota, 2006

Notes: Though the Gizzard Shad is a prolific species across much of its native and introduced range, it is relatively uncommon in Arizona waters, where it is overshadowed by the Threadfin Shad. The name "gizzard" refers to its long, convoluted intestine, which is often packed with sand. It filters plankton, algae and suspended organic matter through its gill rakers, and also "grazes" the bottom for insects and organic sediment. Large Gizzard Shad up to 18 inches in length are sometimes caught with hook and line.

41

Description: silver-blue back fading to white sides and belly; yellow coloration on all fins except dorsal; speckled chin and bottom of mouth

Similar Species: Gizzard Shad (pg. 40)

Threadfin Shad
lower jaw projects past tip of snout

Gizzard Shad
lower jaw does not project past tip of snout

Threadfin Shad
yellow tail

Gizzard Shad
no yellow on tail

THREADFIN SHAD

Dorosoma petenense

Other Names: none

Habitat: open water of large rivers and reservoirs; prefers moderate current in flowing water situations; seeks warm water when temperatures fall, sometimes schooling along shallow, sand shorelines

Range: native west of the Appalachians north to Kentucky, west to Texas, south to the Rio Grand drainage east to Florida; widely introduced; found in many Arizona waters

Food: planktonic algae and crustaceans, some organic matter from bottom

Reproduction: spawns in spring when water hits about 70 degrees F and may continue through summer; schools follow shorelines, spawning near grass clumps, wood or debris; depending on its size, a female typically carries between 800 to 9,000 adhesive eggs, which hatch in 4 to 5 days

Average Size: 4 to 5 inches

Records: none

Notes: Threadfin Shad from Tennessee were released into Lake Mead in 1953 and Havasu in 1954. Within two years they had spread through the entire lower Colorado River system to the delta in Mexico. Shad have also been planted in numerous other Arizona waters and form a large part of the forage base in many systems. Despite their reproductive potential, they are extremely temperature sensitive, and massive die-offs can occur in water colder than 45 degrees.

Description: olive-brown back; sides tan, yellow to black fading to yellowish white underside; sides marked by series of thin, dark bars; broad, flat head; breeding males may turn bright yellow and red

Similar Species: Mosquitofish (pg. 48)

Plains Killifish	Mosquitofish	Plains Killifish	Mosquitofish
vertical bars on sides	sides lack bars	front of dorsal fin slightly ahead of anal fin	anal fin mostly to entirely ahead of dorsal fin

PLAINS KILLIFISH

Plancterus kansae

Other Names: none

Habitat: rivers and shallow streams, often with sand or silt bottom; favors quiet water adjacent to shoals, channels and banks; also found in backwaters; tolerates some current

Range: native to Mississippi River and Gulf Slope drainages from Missouri to Wyoming south to Texas; introduced elsewhere; in Arizona, it is reported from the Colorado and Little Colorado drainages and Lake Powell

Food: aquatic invertebrates, algae

Reproduction: matures at about 2 years; spawns May through July when water temperatures reach 80 degrees F; males do not establish territories but become aggressive toward other males; spawns in pairs, commonly burying eggs in sand bottom

Average Size: 2 to 3 inches

Records: none

Notes: A common species on the western Great Plains but non-native in Arizona, the Plains Killifish can survive water less than an inch deep and tolerate water temperatures approaching 90 degrees. A true diehard, it has been known to survive in areas where farm runoff has left the bottom covered with oxygen-burning organic matter. Lives in loose schools and has been observed burying itself in sand, leaving only its head exposed.

Description: dark back, fading to tan or olive sides with white belly; dark lateral band; short snout; tail round to squared; some breeding males exhibit black coloration

Similar Species: Mosquitofish (pg. 48)

Gila Topminnow	**Mosquitofish**
female lacks spots on tail	female has spots on tail

Gila Topminnow	**Mosquitofish**
front of dorsal fin even with anal fin	front of dorsal fin behind anal fin

Gila Topminnow	**Mosquitofish**
female lacks teardrop marking below eye	female has teardrop mark below eye

GILA TOPMINNOW

Poeciliopsis occidentalis

Other Names: Sonora topminnow

Habitat: springs and weedy shorelines, flats and backwater areas of rivers and streams; prefers warm, shallow water with thick vegetation and algae mat

Range: native to Gila River drainage in Arizona, New Mexico and Mexico below 5,000 feet elevation; in Arizona it is currently found in Gila and Bill Williams drainages

Food: insect larvae, crustaceans, bottom debris, plant matter

Reproduction: gives birth to live young; breeding season January to August; female's eggs are fertilized internally, where young develop; a female may carry several broods at once, at different stages of development, and store sperm for later fertilization; brood size typically 10-15 young

Average Size: males less than 1 inch, females to 2 inches

Records: none

Notes: A hardy fish, it can tolerate water temperatures from near freezing to 100 degrees F, varying degrees of pH and dissolved oxygen, and salinity equal to seawater. Once common in southern Arizona, its numbers have declined due to predation and competition by the non-native species—particularly the Mosquitofish, which devours young topminnows and adult males, and shreds the fins of large adult females, causing infections and death. Even in ideal conditions, they typically do not live more than one year. Young may mature within a few weeks of birth.

47

Description: gray to brown or olive with no bars or bands on sides; rounded tail; flat head; mouth pointed upward

Similar Species: Gila Topminnow (pg. 46), Plains Killifish (Pg. 44)

Mosquitofish
female has spots on tail

Gila Topminnow
female lacks spots on tail

Mosquitofish
female has teardrop mark below eye

Gila Topminnow
female lacks teardrop marking below eye

Mosquitofish
front of dorsal fin behind anal fin

Gila Topminnow
front of dorsal fin even with anal fin

Plains Killifish
front of dorsal slightly ahead of anal fin

MOSQUITOFISH

Gambusia affinis

Other Names: western mosquitofish

Habitat: ponds, oxbows, marshes and backwaters of warm streams and rivers; favors vegetation or other cover, but adapts to a variety of conditions

Range: native to Atlantic and Gulf Slope drainages from southern New Jersey to Mexico, the Mississippi River basin from central Indiana and Illinois to the Gulf; widely introduced; in Arizona, it is found in most warmwater habitats

Food: zooplankton, invertebrates, small fish

Reproduction: gives birth to live young; breeding season lasts 10 to 15 weeks in summer; female may produce 4 broods per year; eggs hatch 21 to 28 days after fertilization

Average Size: males less than 1.2 inches, females 2 inches

Records: none

Notes: An aggressive, non-native predator. First reported in Arizona in 1926, it has spread to most suitable warmwater habitats in the state, severely reducing the populations of native species such as the Gila Topminnow in the process. Ironically, although it is stocked for mosquito control, recent research reviews have not shown it more effective than native pupfish or topminnows in reducing mosquito populations or mosquito-borne diseases. In fact, the Mosquitofish may actually benefit mosquitos by reducing competition with zooplankton and predation from insects and native species that are more efficient mosquito killers.

Description: slate-gray back fading to silver sides and white belly; body often has dark blotches; down-turned eyes set low on head; upturned mouth lacks barbels

Similar Species: Common Carp (pg. 52), Grass Carp (pg. 54)

Bighead Carp   **Common Carp**   **Bighead Carp**   **Grass Carp**

low-set eyes, upturned mouth lacks barbels   eyes high on head; down-turned mouth with barbels   eye below front of upper lip   eye even with or above front of upper lip

Bighead Carp   **Grass Carp**

anal fin 13-14 rays   anal fin 8-10 rays

BIGHEAD CARP

Hypophthalmichthys nobilis

Other Names: Asian carp

Habitat: large, warm rivers and connected lakes; often found in lower sections of tributaries and in flooded areas

Range: southern and central China, widely introduced in U.S.; in Arizona, reported in Kennedy Lake in Tucson

Food: floating plankton and organic matter

Reproduction: spawns from late spring to early summer in warm, flowing water, often in conjunction with increases in current or water level

Average Size: 20 to 30 inches; 12 to 15 pounds

Records: state—none; North American—90 pounds, Kirby Lake, Texas, 2000

Notes: The Bighead Carp is a non-native species that could threaten Arizona's native fish by competing for (or depleting) plankton. The bighead arrived in the U.S. in the early 1970s, imported by a fish farmer hoping to improve water quality. Its discovery in Tucson's Kennedy Lake in early 2007 had state fisheries biologists pleading with anglers to avoid accidentally transporting the species from one lake to another. Emptying bait buckets on land and draining livewells before heading to a new lake are two easy ways to help stop the spread of exotic species such as Bighead Carp.

COMMON CARP

MIRROR CARP

KOI

Description: brassy yellow to golden brown or dark-olive sides; white belly; some red on tail and anal fin; each scale has a dark spot at the base and a dark margin; two pairs of barbels near round, extendable mouth

Similar Species: Bighead Carp (pg. 50), Grass Carp (pg. 54)

Common Carp   **Bighead Carp**   **Grass Carp**

down-turned mouth with barbels

upturned mouth lacks barbels

forward facing mouth lacks barbels

COMMON CARP

Cyprinus carpio

Other Names: German, leather or mirror carp, buglemouth

Habitat: warm, shallow, weedy waters of streams and lakes

Range: native to Asia, widely introduced elsewhere; reported from waters across much of Arizona

Food: prefers insects, crustaceans and mollusks but at times eats algae and other plants

Reproduction: spawns from late February to July in shallow water along stream and lake edges; eggs randomly broadcast over rocks, logs and debris; spawning adults are easily seen due to energetic splashing along shore; female may produce from 100,000 to 2 million eggs

Average Size: 15 to 22 inches, 1 to 7 pounds

Records: state—37 pounds, Bartlett Lake, 1987; North American—57 pounds, 13 ounces, Tidal Basin, Washington D.C., 1983

Notes: A fast-growing Asian minnow, it was introduced in North America as a food fish but has since become considered a pest. It is very prolific and often uproots aquatic plants and increases turbidity (cloudiness) in shallow lakes. The Common Carp arrived in Arizona prior to 1885 and is currently found in most warmwater lakes and rivers, and even some coldwater lakes at higher elevations. Not popular with most anglers, but some fish for it with nymphs, streamers and natural baits. Mirror Carp and Koi (see insets) are varieties of the Common Carp.

Description: gold to olive or silver back fading to yellowish-white underside; thick body; broad, blunt head; large, forward-facing mouth; large, dark-edged scales; low-set eyes

Similar Species: Bighead Carp (pg. 50), Common Carp (pg. 52)

Grass Carp	**Common Carp**	**Grass Carp**	**Bighead Carp**
forward facing mouth lacks barbels	down-turned mouth with barbels	anal fin 8-10 rays	anal fin 13-14 rays

GRASS CARP

Ctenopharyngodon idella

Cyprinidae

Other Names: white amur

Habitat: quiet waters of lakes, ponds, and the pools and backwaters of large rivers

Range: native to eastern Asia from Amur River of eastern Russia and China to the West River in southern China and Thailand; widely introduced in North America; released into some Arizona waters by permit for weed control

Food: aquatic vegetation including filamentous algae

Reproduction: spawns in main-channel areas from late spring to early when water temperatures reach 53 to 63 degrees F; eggs drift with the current and must remain suspended during incubation, which lasts 20 to 40 hours; for this reason, long stretches of flowing water are required

Average Size: 16 to 40 inches, 5 to 50 pounds

Records: state—47 pounds, 1.6 ounces, Encanto Park Lake, 2002; North American—78 pounds, 12 ounces, Flint River, Georgia, 2003

Notes: The Grass Carp is an herbivore (plant eater) with a voracious appetite, known to consume from 40 to 300 percent of its body weight each day. It is also one of the largest members of the minnow family, reportedly reaching lengths of 48 inches and weights well over 100 pounds in its native range. It has been stocked in North America as a food fish and to control aquatic vegetation. Because it eats plants, it is rarely caught on hook and line.

55

Description: gray or olive back; silver sides; white belly; slight bump behind head; caudal peduncle (area ahead of tail) is extremely thin

Similar Species: Humpback Chub (pg. 60)

Bonytail

slight bump behind head

Humpback Chub

pronounced hump behind head

BONYTAIL CHUB

Gila elegans

Cyprinidae

Other Names: bonytail

Habitat: large, swift waters of the Colorado River system

Range: historically found in the Colorado River system, including the Yampa, Gila, Green, Gunnison and Colorado rivers, now limited to the Green River drainage in Utah and Mohave Reservoir in Arizona/Nevada—and perhaps downstream to Parker Dam

Food: insects, zooplankton, algae, plant debris

Reproduction: in Lake Mohave, spawning has been observed in May over a gravel shelf; research in the upper Green River has documented spawning in June and July at water temperatures of around 64 degrees F; eggs are scattered, and there is no parental care

Average Size: 16 to 24 inches

Records: none

Notes: Considered the rarest of the rare Colorado River fish, the federally endangered Bonytail Chub sports large fins and a streamlined body. It has been known to live nearly 50 years. Biologists believe widespread damming of the Colorado reduced critical habitat. Competition from and predation by non-native fish species may also have contributed to its decline. Restoration efforts include the reduction of non-native species, and restocking with hatchery fish, which have been largely unsuccessful.

Description: overall dark coloration, sometimes with light underside; chunky body with large scales; breeding males develop red or orange coloration with yellow-orange eyes

Similar Species: Roundtail Chub (pg. 62)

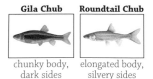

Gila Chub	Roundtail Chub
chunky body, dark sides	elongated body, silvery sides

GILA CHUB
Gila intermedia

Other Names: none

Habitat: small headwater streams, springs and marshes; adults prefer deep pools with weedy shorelines and undercut banks

Range: native to Gila River drainage in Arizona and New Mexico, and possibly the Santa Cruz and San Pedro systems in Sonora, Mexico; in Arizona, currently reported from the Santa Cruz, Middle Gila, San Pedro, Agua Fria and Verde river systems

Food: aquatic and terrestrial insects, fish, algae

Reproduction: thought to mature in second to third year; spawns over vegetation from late spring into summer in streams, but those in springs may spawn into late winter

Average Size: females less than 10 inches, males less than 6 inches

Records: none

Notes: A secretive fish that prefers deep water near cover, the Gila Chub is often found with Gila Topminnows, Desert and Sonora Suckers, and Longfin and Speckled Dace. Adults typically feed early and late in the day. Although its numbers normally rise and fall seasonally and with climate changes, the Gila Chub has been on a gradual decline. It has disappeared from New Mexico and Arizona's Monkey Springs, and the Cave and Fish creek systems.

Description: distinguished by pronounced hump behind the head; greenish back fading to silver sides; white belly; snout overhangs lip

Similar Species: Razorback Sucker (pg. 134)

Humpback Chub	**Razorback Sucker**
pronounced hump behind head	ridge behind head lacks pronounced hump

Humpback Chub	**Razorback Sucker**
9 rays in dorsal fin	13 to 16 rays in dorsal fin

HUMPBACK CHUB

Gila cypha

Other Names: humpback

Habitat: turbulent, fast-flowing, deep, turbid (cloudy) water, often associated with cliffs, boulders and canyons

Range: historically throughout the Colorado River system from the Green River in Wyoming to the mouth of the Grand Canyon; in Arizona, the Colorado and Little Colorado rivers in the Grand Canyon

Food: small insects, algae, sometimes fish

Reproduction: spawns April through July during high water periods; captive fish have spawned over bottom composed of small rocks and boulders

Average Size: 12 to 16 inches, 12 ounces to 2 pounds

Records: none

Notes: A remarkable and striking member of the minnow family, the Humpback Chub is a federally Endangered Species. Once common throughout the Colorado River system in and upstream of the Grand Canyon, its populations declined due to dam construction and water diversion projects—which lower water temperatures and block migrations Restoration efforts include the removal of non-native fish. Though it inhabits whitewater canyons, it lacks the speed and strength of the Colorado Pikeminnow. Rather, it relies on its large fins to glide through slow-water areas as it feeds.

Description: dark olive-gray back fading to silver sides; large mouth; lower lip has black outline; slight hump on back above gill flap; large, forked tail with slender base

Similar Species: Bonytail Chub (pg. 56), Humpback Chub (pg. 60)

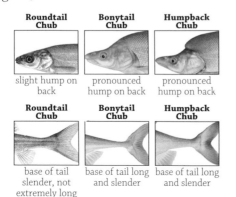

Roundtail Chub	Bonytail Chub	Humpback Chub
slight hump on back	pronounced hump on back	pronounced hump on back
Roundtail Chub	Bonytail Chub	Humpback Chub
base of tail slender, not extremely long	base of tail long and slender	base of tail long and slender

ROUNDTAIL CHUB
Gila robusta

Other Names: Colorado River and round-tailed chub, Gila or Verde trout

Habitat: eddies and pools of cool- to warmwater streams and rivers, often with cover such as fallen timber, rootwads, large rocks or undercut banks; also found in reservoirs

Range: Colorado River basin from Wyoming to Arizona and New Mexico, also northwestern Mexico; in Arizona, throughout the Verde River, the mainstem Salt River and tributaries, canals in Phoenix and a variety of watersheds in the central portion of the state

Food: aquatic and terrestrial insects, filamentous algae, fish

Reproduction: spawns in spring and early summer when spring runoff subsides; female randomly scatters eggs over gravel, often near woody cover; no parental care

Average Size: up to 19 inches

Records: state—3 pounds, 14.9 ounces, Lower Salt River, 1984 (not registered as a North American record); North American—2 pounds, 5 ounces, Verde River, Arizona, 1983

Notes: A member of the minnow family, the Roundtail Chub is a native species popular with anglers. It prefers flowing water and is often found in pools and eddies. Often schools in fast, swirling water below rapids. Roundtails hit artificial lures such as small spinners, spoons and flies— as well as natural baits. They put up a strong fight and are fun to catch on light gear. The firm, white flesh has a mild flavor.

Description: overall dark coloration on upper body, with dark lateral bands and light lateral line; sides and belly lighter; round spot at base of tail; breeding fish may develop red at bases of anal and paired fins

Similar Species: Gila Chub (pg. 58)

Sonora Chub	Gila Chub
round spot at tail base	lacks round spot at tail base

Cyprinidae

SONORA CHUB

Gila ditaenia

Other Names: none

Habitat: deep, permanent pools; undercut banks; often found over bedrock or sand substrate

Range: Rio de la Concepcion drainage of Sonora, Mexico and Arizona; in Arizona, Sycamore Creek (Bear Canyon), two tributaries and one unnamed stream

Food: aquatic and terrestrial insects, algae

Reproduction: the spawn is not believed linked to a particular season, but rather timed to follow spring and summer rains; adults showing breeding coloration have been reported from April through November

Average Size: less than 5 inches in U.S. headwater areas, larger in Mexico

Records: none

Notes: One of Arizona's unique, rare native fish, the Sonora Chub is found in Sycamore Creek west of Nogales in Bear Canyon. It is a hardy survivor capable of enduring droughts in isolated pools, hiding in the shade of undercut banks. A tiny population of dwarfed chubs was once found in a seep containing only a few liters of water; the waterhole was clogged with weedgrowth where it was not trampled by livestock.

Description: dark back with silvery coloration on sides, fading to white belly; 9 or 10 rays in dorsal, anal and pelvic fins; back, breast and portion of belly feature small, deeply embedded scales—"naked" in some individuals

Similar Species: Woundfin (pg. 94)

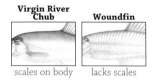

Virgin River Chub — scales on body   Woundfin — lacks scales

VIRGIN RIVER CHUB

Cyprinidae

Gila seminuda

Other Names: Virgin Chub, Virgin Roundtail Chub

Habitat: deep, swift but not turbulent water in the main-stem Virgin River, rarely in tributary mouths; prefers protected areas with boulders of other cover such as rootwads; prefers water temperatures of 75 degrees F

Range: limited to the Virgin River system in northwestern Arizona, southern Nevada and southwestern Utah

Food: an opportunistic omnivore that feeds on algae, aquatic insects, zooplankton and debris

Reproduction: spawns in late spring and early summer over rock or gravel bottom; eggs hatch in a week or less, with no parental care

Average Size: less than 6 inches

Records: none

Notes: A rare native species, the Virgin River Chub is found only in the Virgin River system. Its numbers have declined dramatically due to water flow alterations and the introduction of non-native fish. Rarely exceeds 10 inches in length but known to reach 18 inches.

Description: olive to silvery gray back and upper sides fading to white belly; may have gold spots on sides; lateral stripe ends in spot at base of tail; barbel on each side of upper lip

Similar Species: Fathead Minnow (pg. 74), Mexican Stoneroller (pg. 80)

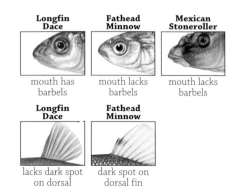

Longfin Dace	Fathead Minnow	Mexican Stoneroller
mouth has barbels	mouth lacks barbels	mouth lacks barbels

Longfin Dace	Fathead Minnow
lacks dark spot on dorsal	dark spot on dorsal fin

LONGFIN DACE

Agosia chrysogaster

Other Names: Gila Longfin Dace

Habitat: eddies and pools of small to mid-size streams ranging from hot, low-desert waterways to clear brooks at higher elevations (typically under 5,000 feet); often found in water less than 1 foot deep, over sand or gravel bottom, near overhanging banks or other cover

Range: Bill Williams, Gila and Rio de la Concepcion drainages in Arizona; introduced in New Mexico; also found in the Rio Sonoyta watershed in Mexico

Food: decaying plant and animal matter, aquatic invertebrates, zooplankton, algae

Reproduction: spawns year-round but mostly December through July; eggs are deposited and buried in saucer-shaped nest, usually located on sand bottom in 2 to 4 inches of water with slight current; eggs hatch in about 4 days

Average Size: up to 2½ inches

Records: none

Notes: Considered the hardiest native minnow, the Longfin Dace tolerates a variety of conditions. In desert streams, it survives droughts and other low-water periods by hiding under algae mats, stones or logs. After heavy rains, it quickly moves back into once-dry streambeds and other suitable habitat. It is vulnerable to predation by non-native fish and crayfish.

69

Description: color varies from dusky yellow or olive with large black blotches to olive or grayish on back, fading to lighter underside; black spot at base of tail; small eye; usually barbels at corners of upper lips

Similar Species: Fathead Minnow (pg. 74), Longfin Dace (pg. 68)

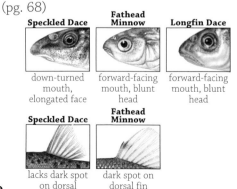

Speckled Dace	**Fathead Minnow**	**Longfin Dace**
down-turned mouth, elongated face	forward-facing mouth, blunt head	forward-facing mouth, blunt head

Speckled Dace	**Fathead Minnow**
lacks dark spot on dorsal	dark spot on dorsal fin

SPECKLED DACE
Rhinichthys osculus

Cyprinidae

Other Names: dusky, Pacific, spring or western dace

Habitat: tolerates habitat from desert springs to mountain streams and lakes; prefers clear, well-oxygenated water with current or wave action; deep-water cover such as woody debris or weedgrowth

Range: native to western North America from Columbia drainage in British Columbia to Colorado River south to Sonora, Mexico; in Arizona, the Colorado, Bill Williams and Gila drainages with the exception of slow, warm sections of the mainstem Colorado

Food: aquatic insects, zooplankton, algae

Reproduction: spawns in spring and again in late summer in riffles or gravelly areas of stream or along lake shorelines; eggs are broadcast on coarse bottom, hatch in about 6 days

Average Size: 3 to 4 inches

Records: none

Notes: This small, native Arizona minnow is an adaptable species, able to survive in a variety of habitats ranging from desert springs to mountain headwaters. Two major body forms: small, speckled variety in the southern Gila River system and larger, banded, nearly uniformly colored version found north of the Mogollon Rim. A schooling fish most active at night. Where common, it is an important forage for game fish.

71

Description: grayish green to bronze back; silver to white sides and belly; fins may develop an orange coloration on breeding fish

Similar Species: Humpback Chub (pg. 60)

Colorado Pikeminnow

lacks hump behind head

Humpback Chub

pronounced hump behind head

COLORADO PIKEMINNOW

Cyprinidae

Ptychocheilus lucius

Other Names: Colorado squawfish, Colorado salmon, white salmon

Habitat: fast-flowing, muddy rivers with warm backwaters

Range: native to the Colorado River basin and main tributaries from Wyoming to Arizona and California

Food: mostly fish, also insects, other invertebrates

Reproduction: adults migrate up to 200 miles to spawning areas such as riffles with gravel or rocky bottoms; spawns during spring and summer; eggs are broadcast randomly, there is no parental care; eggs hatch in less than a week

Average Size: up to 48 inches and 60 pounds

Records: none

Notes: The Colorado Pikeminnow is the largest of North America's native minnows, historically reaching lengths of 5 to 6 feet and weights up to 80 pounds. It is a voracious predator, though its only teeth are found in a bony structure deep in the throat. Once abundant enough to support commercial fishing, it is now rare. Considered extirpated in Arizona, though experimental populations have been introduced in the Salt and Verde drainages, and both adults and juveniles have been found in Lake Powell (though not in Arizona waters). Biologists blame the decline on dam construction and water diversion projects —which blocked access to spawning areas and lowered water temperatures— along with the introduction of non-native fish.

73

NON-SPAWNING ADULT

SPAWNING MALE

Description: olive back, golden yellow sides and white belly; dark lateral line widens to spot at base of tail; rounded snout and fins; no scales on head; dark blotch on dorsal fin

Similar Species: Longfin Dace (pg. 68)

Fathead Minnow	Longfin Dace	Fathead Minnow	Longfin Dace
small mouth; eye centered on head	large mouth; eye high on head	first dorsal ray short, split from other rays	first dorsal ray not split from other rays

FATHEAD MINNOW

Pimephales promelas

Cyprinidae

Other Names: blackhead, mudminnow, tuffy

Habitat: streams, ponds and lakes, particularly shallow, weedy or turbid (cloudy) areas lacking predators

Range: native to much of North America from Quebec to the Northwest Territories south to Alabama, Texas and New Mexico; widely introduced; widespread in Arizona

Food: primarily algae and other plant matter, but will eat insects and copepods

Reproduction: from the time water temperatures reach 65 degrees F in spring through September (unless they surpass 85 degrees), male prepares nest under rocks and sticks; female enters, turns upside down and lays adhesive eggs on the overhead object; after the female leaves, the male fertilizes the eggs, which it then guards, fans with its fins and massages with a special, mucus-like pad on its back

Average Size: 3 to 4 inches

Records: none

Notes: A widespread fish commonly used as bait, the Fathead Minnow is hardy and withstands high temperatures and low oxygen levels. Prior to spawning, the male develops a dark coloration, breeding tubercles on its head and a mucus-like patch on its back; during this phase, anglers report having better luck when using female fatheads, perhaps due to their color or differing scent. Some biologists believe it may threaten native fish populations.

FERAL GOLDFISH

RELEASED GOLDFISH

Description: back and upper sides dark olive-brown fading to yellow below; long dorsal fin; stocky, compressed body

Similar Species: Common Carp (pg. 52), Grass Carp (pg. 54)

Goldfish	**Common Carp**	**Goldfish**	**Grass Carp**
forward facing mouth lacks barbels	down-turned mouth with barbels	dorsal fin 15-19 rays	dorsal fin 7-9 rays

GOLDFISH
Carassius auratus

Other Names: none

Habitat: ponds and the shallow bays of lakes; pools and backwater areas of streams and rivers

Range: non-native to North America but widely introduced across the continent, including Arizona

Food: algae and other plant matter, insects, crustaceans

Reproduction: matures at 1 to 3 years; spawns in late spring and summer, scattering adhesive eggs over submerged vegetation, roots or other objects; female may produce 400,000 eggs, which hatch in 5 to 6 days

Average Size: up to 16 inches and 3½ pounds

Records: state—none; North American—3 pounds, 2 ounces, Lourdes Pond, Indiana, 2002

Notes: Non-native, the Goldfish is widely introduced in Arizona due to releases of bait and aquarium fish. Those released from fish bowls and minnow buckets are typically orange or red in color, but second-generation "wild" or feral Goldfish often lose this trademark coloration and look very similar to Common Carp. Spawning patterns are also similar to Common Carp, making hybrids common in waters where both species are well established.

Description: cryptic coloration is olive green on back with dark blotches and speckles on sides; white underside; elongated body is slightly compressed and flattened vertically; small mouth faces nearly straight forward; breeding males develop bright reddish-orange fin bases, while breeding females exhibit yellowish fins and lower body

Similar Species: Speckled Dace (pg. 70)

Loach Minnow   Speckled Dace

white spots on front and rear of dorsal fin and base of tail

lacks white spots on front and rear of dorsal fin and base of tail

LOACH MINNOW

Tiaroga cobitis

Other Names: none

Habitat: mainstem rivers and tributaries; found in relatively shallow, rocky, turbulent riffles with moderate to swift current and gravel or cobble bottom

Range: historically found in the Gila River Basin of Arizona and in New Mexico and Sonora, Mexico; currently found in limited reaches of the Black, Blue, San Francisco and White rivers and Aravaipa, Campbell Blue and Eagle creeks

Food: insects, mainly larvae of various diptera species

Reproduction: matures at 1 year of age; spawns in riffles from March to June; deposits adhesive eggs on the underside of flattened rocks; male (and possibly female) guards nest cavities that are typically located on the downstream side of rocks; eggs hatch in 5 to 6 days

Average Size: rarely more than 2.6 inches

Records: none

Notes: Because of its reduced gas bladder, this solitary and often sedentary minnow is almost exclusively a bottom dweller. An insect hunter (insectivore), it prefers to pursue prey among bottom substrate, as opposed to chasing dinner higher in the water column. Rarely found where fine sediment fills narrow gaps between rocks and gravel. Once found in more than 1,200 miles of Arizona streams, it is today limited to less than 200 stream miles due to habitat destruction and predation by non-native fish species.

79

Description: back dark gray to olive, fading on sides with
scattered dark spots and dark lateral band; white belly; large
head with rounded snout and small mouth; lower jaw has
hard, shelf-like extension; moderately stout body; breeding
males develop darkened and orange areas on dorsal fin

Similar Species: Longfin Dace (pg. 68)

Mexican Stoneroller	**Longfin Dace**
hard extension in jaw; mouth lacks barbels	jaw lacks hard extension; barbels on mouth

MEXICAN STONEROLLER

Campostoma ornatum

Other Names: none

Habitat: riffles, runs and areas of pools with some current; prefers bottom of gravel or small rocks in riffles and runs, sand or gravel in pools, and undercut banks or other cover

Range: Rio Yaqui drainage of Mexico, east to tributaries of the Rio Grande River, near the Big Bend region of Texas, south through Sonora, Chihuahua and Durango, Mexico; in Arizona, Rucker Canyon in the Chiricahua Mountains and San Bernardino Creek

Food: plant debris, algae, aquatic insects

Reproduction: not well-documented; some sources report spawning activities from winter through late spring; male excavates long, pit-type nest; breeding males develop horn-like tubercles on the head, which are used to defend the nest and stimulate spawning behavior in females; non-adhesive eggs are defended by the male until hatching

Average Size: up to 5 inches

Records: none

Notes: An interesting little native minnow, the Mexican Stoneroller uses an odd, blade-like extension of the lower jaw to scrape algae and other plant matter from rocks, logs and other objects on the bottom. Related Central Stoneroller (*Campostoma anomalum*) has been known to form large schools, which can be observed swirling in pools and runs as the fish "graze" the bottom.

81

Description: back orange or yellow; body bluish; top of head red to orange; pointed snout; compressed body

Similar Species: Red Shiner (pg. 86)

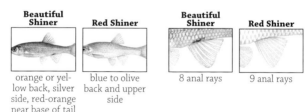

Beautiful Shiner	Red Shiner	Beautiful Shiner	Red Shiner
orange or yellow back, silver side, red-orange near base of tail	blue to olive back and upper side	8 anal rays	9 anal rays

BEAUTIFUL SHINER

Cyprinella formosa

Other Names: Yaqui Shiner, Guzman Beautiful Shiner

Habitat: pools of streams with gravel, rock or sandy bottom; also found in riffles of small streams and intermittent pools in creeks with numerous riffles in high-water periods

Range: Rio Yaqui drainage in Arizona, Mimbres River, New Mexico, and Sonora and Chihuahua, Mexico; in Arizona, San Bernardino National Wildlife Refuge

Food: aquatic and terrestrial insects

Reproduction: spawning not well-documented; believed to spawn May to July, spreading eggs over vegetation, submerged branches and other cover or open bottom

Average Size: up to 3½ inches

Records: none

Notes: The Beautiful Shiner is a rare, native species at risk due to habitat loss and non-native fish and bullfrogs. More than 700 fish were caught in Mexico and transported to Dexter National Fish Hatchery in New Mexico to establish a captive breeding program. Re-introduced into the San Bernardino National Wildlife Refuge in May of 1990.

Description: olive green back fading to golden or silvery sides; silver-white belly; deep body; small, upturned mouth; scaleless keel on belly behind pelvic fins; breeding males may develop orange-red tail

Similar Species: Red Shiner (pg. 86)

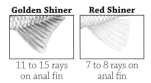

Golden Shiner	Red Shiner
11 to 15 rays on anal fin	7 to 8 rays on anal fin

GOLDEN SHINER
Notemigonus crysoleucas

Other Names: none

Habitat: ponds, lakes, sloughs and slack-water pools in slow-flowing streams; does well in heavy weedgrowth; tolerates moderately turbid (cloudy) water

Range: central and eastern North America, including Atlantic, Gulf Slope, Great Lakes and Mississippi River basins from Nova Scotia to Alberta south to Texas and Florida; widely introduced, including Arizona

Food: plant and animal matter ranging from algae and higher vegetation to crustaceans, insects and snails

Reproduction: spawns in spring and early summer at water temperatures of 70 to 80 degrees F; may spawn again in late summer; no nest; female scatters adhesive eggs over vegetation, filamentous algae or nests of other fish such as Largemouth Bass; eggs hatch in 4 days

Average Size: 3 to 6 inches

Records: none

Notes: Widely distributed outside its native range due to its status as a bait- and ornamental fish, the Golden Shiner often gathers in loose schools that can be found from near the surface down to the middle of the water column. Some studies have linked the arrival of Golden Shiner to decreased growth and reproduction in trout due to competition for food and space. Shiners may also compete for food with juvenile bass and sunfish.

85

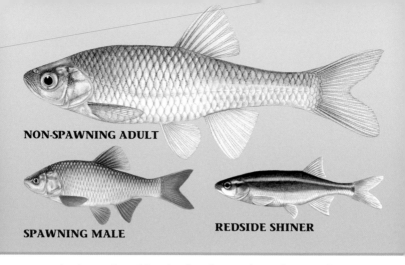

NON-SPAWNING ADULT

SPAWNING MALE

REDSIDE SHINER

Description: silver-blue back, silver sides; white underside; breeding males develop metallic blue coloration with bright orange-red on the head and fins (except dorsal)

Similar Species: Redside Shiner

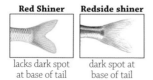

Red Shiner	Redside shiner
lacks dark spot at base of tail	dark spot at base of tail

RED SHINER
Cyprinella lutrensis

Other Names: none

Habitat: clear to silty water with fluctuating flows

Range: mid- to southwestern U.S. from Wisconsin and Indiana west to Colorado, south to Louisiana, Texas and Mexico; widely introduced; in Arizona, the Colorado River system, including major tributaries

Food: an opportunist, eats a variety of algae and other plant matter, invertebrates and other small food items

Reproduction: spawns through spring and summer at water temperatures from 60 to 65 degrees F; will spawn in a variety of areas—in vegetation and woody cover, over sand and gravel bottoms, even along the edges of nests of other fish (such as Bluegills)

Average Size: up to 3 inches

Records: none

Notes: A schooling fish that spends much of its time in the middle of the water column or near the surface, the Red Shiner can tolerate pollution better than many species. It prefers backwater areas and deep pools where current speeds are less than one foot per second. Nationally, its range has expanded thanks to the bait and aquarium trade. Research has shown this highly adaptable fish easily colonizes new areas and hybridizes with "local" shiner species, threatening native fish populations. Similar in appearance to non-native Redside Shiner found in northwest Arizona.

Description: olive, gray or bluish back with silvery sides; belly white to yellowish; lateral blotches are rare; strong second "spine" in dorsal

Similar Species: Spikedace (pg. 90)

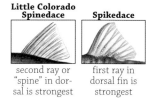

Little Colorado Spinedace

second ray or "spine" in dorsal is strongest

Spikedace

first ray in dorsal fin is strongest

LITTLE COLORADO SPINEDACE

Cyprinidae

Lepidomeda vittata

Other Names: Little Colorado River Spinedace

Habitat: small to medium-size streams at elevations from 4,000 to 8,000 feet; prefers water temperatures of 58 to 79 degrees F in pools with rocks or undercut banks and slow to moderate current over fine gravel bottom; avoids deep, shady pools and shallows lacking cover

Range: Little Colorado River and north-flowing tributaries, possibly Zuni River system in New Mexico; in Arizona, the mainstem Little Colorado River and Chevelon, Clear and Nutrioso creeks

Food: aquatic and terrestrial insects

Reproduction: spawns early summer through early fall; female broadcasts 650 to 5,000 eggs over bottom or on weedgrowth or debris

Average Size: less than 4 inches

Records: none

Notes: A tenacious Arizona native, the Little Colorado Spinedace tolerates harsh environmental conditions and fluctuations in water temperature, dissolved gas and pH levels. It survives droughts in deep pools or spring areas, then spreads throughout stream when water returns. Its numbers have declined due to habitat loss, fish poisons and the introduction of non-native crayfish and fish species such as Rainbow Trout and Green Sunfish.

Description: olive-gray to light brown back; bright silver sides, commonly with bluish reflections; dark specks and blotches on upper sides and back; slender body; spawning male develops striking brassy-yellow head and fins

Similar Species: Woundfin (pg. 94)

Spikedace   **Woundfin**

mouth lacks   barbels at
barbels   corners of
                  mouth

SPIKEDACE

Meda fulgida

Other Names: none

Habitat: medium-size to large streams with permanent flows; prefers less than 3 feet deep with sand, rubble or gravel bottom; often found in the downstream ends of riffles, current "seams" between fast and slow flows, and the upper sections of gravel or sand bars in the main channel; concentrates at tributary mouths in larger streams

Range: upper Gila River basin of Arizona and New Mexico; in Arizona, currently found in small sections of Aravaipa and Eagle creeks and 35 miles of the Verde River

Food: aquatic and terrestrial insects, fry of other fish species

Reproduction: spawns in spring and summer; males patrol shallow, sand- or gravel-bottom areas with modest current; female enters area from downstream and is joined by 2 or more males; after a brief "chase," spawning occurs; female deposits 100 to 300 eggs

Average Size: 1½ to 2½ inches

Records: none

Notes: This Arizona native owes its intimidating name to the sharp spiny ray of its dorsal fin. Unfortunately, the Spikedace was unable to fend off predation by and competition with non-native fish, or the effects of habitat loss. Like many native fish, its populations and range have declined. Restoration of natural flooding and exotic species control are thought to be keys to its future success.

91

Description: dark back; silvery sides, often with dark speckles on upper body (may extend below lateral line) and brassy reflections; large eye; rounded head

Similar Species: Little Colorado Spinedace (pg. 88)

Virgin Spinedace	**Little Colorado Spinedace**	**Virgin Spinedace**	**Little Colorado Spinedace**
usually 9 anal fin rays	usually 8 anal fin rays	fewer than 90 scales in lateral line	more than 90 scales in lateral line

Cyprinidae

VIRGIN SPINEDACE

Lepidomeda mollispinis mollispinis

Other Names: Virgin River Spinedace

Habitat: cool, clear, swift-flowing streams with mix of riffles, runs and pools; favors pools with protective cover such as boulders, undercut banks or debris; also found in narrow runs with thick weedgrowth

Range: Virgin River system in Arizona, Nevada and Utah; in Arizona, lower Beaver Dam Wash and portions of the Virgin River, once found in Virgin River from Utah border to Littlefield

Food: insects, plant matter, organic debris

Reproduction: matures at about 1 year; spawns from spring through early summer at water temperatures of 55 to 62 degrees F when there are more than 13 hours of daylight per day; female typically produces from 450 to nearly 800 eggs, depending on her age

Average Size: 2½ to 4½ inches

Records: none

Notes: Mainly insect eaters, spinedace often prowl the middle of the water column, occasionally darting to the surface to capture prey. They will feed off bottom, however, and eat algae when other insects are scarce. Average life span is 3 years. In addition to the habitat types above, researchers have documented a preference for the "seam" between swift and nearly slack current.

Description: overall silver coloration; pectoral fins may be watery yellow; has dermal "plates" instead of scales; flattened head and belly; small mouth with barbel in corners; 2 spines in dorsal fin

Similar Species: Spikedace (pg. 90), Little Colorado Spinedace (pg. 88), Virgin Spinedace (pg. 92)

Woundfin — barbels at corners of mouth

Spikedace — mouth lacks barbels

Woundfin — lacks scales

Spinedace — scales on body

WOUNDFIN
Plagopterus argentissimus

Other Names: none

Habitat: main channel areas of warm, seasonally fast-flowing streams with shifting sand bottom; tolerates extremely turbid (cloudy) and mineralized water; prefers water depths of 8 to 18 inches; seldom found in pools or clear water

Range: historically the lower Colorado River basin including Gila, Moapa, Salt and Virgin river systems; currently reported in only about 50 miles of Virgin River in Arizona, Nevada and Utah; in Arizona, the Virgin River mainstem

Food: filamentous algae, organic debris, seeds, aquatic insects

Reproduction: matures by second summer; spawns April to July as spring flows decline; eggs deposited in swift shallows over gravel bottom; fry appear from June throughout summer

Average Size: up to 3 inches

Records: none

Notes: Despite its diminutive size, the Woundfin has an intimidating name, no doubt in acknowledgement of the spines in its dorsal fin. Known to make long downstream migrations and thrive in swift-flowing warm, cloudy water. Eliminated from most of historic range due to habitat loss and non-native species. Found sporadically through Arizona's portion of the Virgin River mainstem in Mohave County.

Description: blue-black back fading to silver sides and silvery-white belly; small, forward-facing mouth; dark spot at base of pectoral fins, which are set high on sides; no visible lateral line

Similar Species: Pacific Tenpounder (pg. 162)

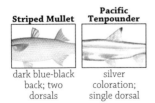

Striped Mullet	Pacific Tenpounder
dark blue-black back; two dorsals	silver coloration; single dorsal

STRIPED MULLET

Mugil cephalus

Other Names: none

Habitat: fresh-, brackish (slightly salty) and saltwater habitats in depths to nearly 400 feet; prefers water temperatures from 46 to 75 F; often schools over sand or mud bottoms

Range: coastal areas, river mouths and estuaries worldwide between 42 degrees N and 42 degrees S latitude; in Arizona, currently found in the Colorado River below Laguna Dam and lower Gila River, often found in canals in this region

Food: zooplankton, crustaceans, algae, organic debris

Reproduction: males mature at age 3, females mature at age 4; spawns in open sea; reproduction in Colorado River uncertain

Average Size: up to 23 inches and 8 pounds

Records: state—9 pounds, 8 ounces, Colorado/Gila River confluence, 1976

Notes: One of two saltwater fish endemic to Arizona, the Striped Mullet is found in small groups in larger pools of the Colorado River, sometimes moving into current areas below dams. Populations are declining because young mullet only move into Arizona when the Colorado River reaches the Sea of Cortez. Adults known to reach sizes of nearly 50 inches and 20 pounds.

Description: silver or golden to dark olive brown in color; sharp canine teeth; dark spot at base of the three last spines in the dorsal fin; white spot on bottom lobe of tail

Similar Species: Yellow Perch

Walleye	**Yellow Perch**
prominent white spot on bottom lobe of tail	no prominent white spot on bottom lobe of tail

WALLEYE
Sander vitreus

Other Names: marble-eyes, walleyed pike, jack, pickerel

Habitat: large lakes, reservoirs and rivers

Range: originally northern U.S. and Canada, now widely introduced; in Arizona, lakes including Apache, Canyon, Fool's Hollow, Mary, Powell, Saguaro and Show Low

Food: mainly small fish such as Threadfin Shad and various minnows; also eats insects, crayfish, leeches

Reproduction: matures at 2 to 4 years; spawns at night in tributary streams or wind- or current-washed lake shoals when spring water temperatures reach 40 to 50 degrees F; prefers rubble bottom in shallow water; groups of adults broadcast eggs, which typically hatch in 12 to 18 days

Average Size: 14 to 20 inches, 1 to 3 pounds

Records: state—16 pounds, 1.76 ounces, Show Low Lake, 2002; North American—22 pounds, 11 ounces, Greer's Ferry Lake, Arkansas, 1982

Notes: Introduced to Arizona in 1957. Puts up a good fight and its white fillets rank extremely high in table quality. Thanks to a reflective layer of pigment in the eye—called tapetum lucidum— the Walleye can see well in low-light conditions. This gives it an advantage over species that have poor night vision or cannot quickly adapt to reduced light levels. Walleyes exploit this advantage by feeding at dusk, dawn, night and in light-reducing conditions such as waves, disturbed sediment or thick cloud cover

Description: 6 to 9 dark, vertical bars on bright yellowish green to orange background; long dorsal with two distinct lobes; lower fins have a yellow to orange tinge

Similar Species: Walleye (pg. 98)

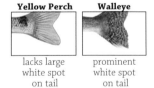

Yellow Perch	Walleye
lacks large white spot on tail	prominent white spot on tail

Percidae

YELLOW PERCH

Perca flavescens

Other Names: ringed, striped or jack perch, green hornet

Habitat: warm to cool lakes and slow-flowing streams, adults prefer clear open water

Range: native to Atlantic, Arctic, Great Lakes and Mississippi drainages from southern Canada through North Dakota south and east to Georgia; widely introduced elsewhere, including Arizona

Food: small fish, insects, snails, leeches and crayfish

Reproduction: matures at 2 years; spawns at night in shallow, weedy areas in spring when water warms to 45 to 50 degrees F; female drapes gelatinous ribbons of eggs over submerged vegetation; eggs incubate 10 to 20 days

Average Size: 8 to 11 inches, 6 to 10 ounces

Records: state—1 pound, 10 ounces, Stoneman Lake, 1984; North American—4 pounds, 3 ounces, Bordentown, New Jersey, 1865

Notes: A non-native species that came to Arizona in 1919, the Yellow Perch has a rollercoaster history in the state. In the 1930s large populations were reported in some high-elevation lakes in central Arizona, and the species has sporadically popped up elsewhere. Currently, Stoneman Lake offers the best chance at sighting or catching perch. Excellent table quality. Within their native range, perch are an important link in the food web. However, illegally stocked Yellow Perch can harm some native species.

Description: long body with dorsal fin near tail; head is long and flattened in front, forming a duck-like snout; dark green back, light green sides with bean-shaped light spots; Silver Pike are a rare, silver colored race of Northern Pike

Similar Species: Colorado Pikeminnow (pg. 72), Walleye (pg. 98)

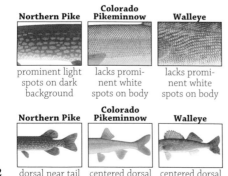

Northern Pike	Colorado Pikeminnow	Walleye
prominent light spots on dark background	lacks prominent white spots on body	lacks prominent white spots on body

Northern Pike	Colorado Pikeminnow	Walleye
dorsal near tail	centered dorsal	centered dorsal

NORTHERN PIKE

Esox lucius

Other Names: pickerel, jack, 'gator, hammerhandle, snot rocket

Habitat: lakes, streams and rivers (avoids strong currents); often found near weeds but will range open water; small pike tolerate water temperatures up to 70 degrees F but larger fish prefer 55 degrees or less

Range: northern Europe, Asia and North America; in Arizona, introduced in a number of lakes and ponds including Ashurst, Long, Mary, Mormon and Stoneman lakes

Food: small fish, frogs, crayfish and other small creatures; typically feeds on live prey but will scavenge dead fish

Reproduction: spawns late March into April in tributaries and marshes at 34- to 40-degree water temperatures; attended by 1 to 3 males, female deposits eggs in vegetation; eggs hatch in about 14 days

Average Size: 18 to 24 inches, 2 to 5 pounds

Records: state—32 pounds, 5.6 ounces, Ashurst Lake, 2004; North American—46 pounds, 2 ounces, Sacandaga Reservoir, New York, 1940

Notes: A non-native species that arrived in Arizona in 1965, the Northern Pike is a voracious predator and prized sportfish in its native range. However when stocked into new fisheries it can put a dent in native fish populations. Eagerly hits natural and artificial baits and fights hard when hooked. A daytime sight feeder, it often lies in wait in weedy cover, capturing prey with a fast lunge.

Description: silver with narrow, dark vertical bars on sides; breeding males develop yellow, orange or reddish coloration on tail area with light-blue body; upturned mouth; rounded dorsal fin

Similar Species: similar in appearance to Quitobaquito Pupfish (not shown), which is found only in Organ Pipe Cactus National Monument and a nearby concrete tank

DESERT PUPFISH

Cyprinodon macularius

Other Names: pupfish

Habitat: springs, marshes, streams, river backwaters; appears to prefer clear, shallow water and soft bottom

Range: lower Colorado and Gila river systems in Arizona and Baja California, Salton Sea and tributaries in California, and Sonora, Mexico; in Arizona, natural populations thought to be eliminated; restoration efforts include Cold Springs in Graham County and Finley Tank in Santa Cruz County

Food: algae, small pieces of aquatic plants, mosquito larvae and other small invertebrates, organic debris

Reproduction: may reach sexual maturity in as little as 6 weeks; spawns in spring and early summer; breeding males become territorial and aggressive; female randomly deposits eggs in male's territory; by patrolling his territory, the male inadvertently guards eggs, which hatch in several days

Average Size: 2 to 3 inches

Records: none

Notes: Once common but now eliminated from most of its historical range due to habitat loss and introduction of non-native species. Reportedly able to survive water temperatures more than 95 degrees F and salt concentrations nearly three times higher than sea water. Despite this hardiness, they rarely live longer than 1 year. May dig and then defend pits while seeking food.

Description: dark olive back and tip of head; yellowish-gold body; dark spots on tail and dorsal; white-tipped dorsal, pelvic and anal fins; scattered dark spots on body may extend below lateral line; small dark spots on either side of pupil; may have orange or yellow slash mark on throat

Similar Species: Cutthroat Trout (pg. 112), Rainbow Trout (pg. 116)

Apache Trout

dots on either side of pupil; may have orange or yellow mark on throat

Cutthroat Trout

lacks dots on either side of pupil; red stripe on throat

Rainbow Trout

lacks dots on either side of pupil; lacks stripe on throat

106

APACHE TROUT

Oncorhynchus apache

Salmonidae

Other Names: Arizona trout, yellow belly

Habitat: clear, cool, high-elevation rivers and streams

Range: found in the Upper Salt and Little Colorado drainages of Arizona's White Mountains

Food: aquatic and terrestrial insects

Reproduction: matures at 3 years; spawns March through mid-June, depending on elevation, when water temperature reaches 46 degrees F; spawning bed or "redd" is located at lower end of pool; eggs hatch in 30 days and young fish leave redd 30 days after that

Average Size: 6 to 24 inches, 6 ounces to more than 5 pounds

Records: state and North American—5 pounds, 15.5 ounces, Hurricane Lake, 1993

Notes: A beautiful Arizona native and the official state fish, the Apache Trout is one of two trout originally found in the state. Once very abundant in White Mountain streams, it was pushed to near extinction by habitat degradation, competition from non-native species and overfishing. Recovery efforts have restored the Apache Trout in much of its original range, and fishing is allowed in select waters. A willing striker, it hits artificial flies as well as worms or salmon eggs. Its firm, flaky fillets have excellent table qualities.

Description: back is olive, blue-gray to black with worm-like markings; sides bronze to olive with red spots tinged light brown; lower fins red-orange with white leading edge; tail squared or slightly forked

Similar Species: Apache Trout (pg. 106), Brown Trout (pg. 110), Rainbow Trout (pg. 116)

Brook Trout	**Apache Trout**	**Brown Trout**	**Rainbow Trout**
worm-like marks	lacks worm-like marks on back	lacks worm-like marks on back	lacks worm-like marks on back

BROOK TROUT
Salvelinus fontinalis

Other Names: speckled, squaretail or coaster trout, brookie

Habitat: cool, clear streams and lakes; prefers sand or gravel bottoms, moderate vegetation and water temperatures of 50 to 60 degrees F

Range: Great Lakes region north to Labrador, south through the Appalachians to Georgia; introduced into the western U.S., Canada, Europe and South America; found in the White Mountains in Arizona

Food: insects, small fish, leeches, crustaceans

Reproduction: spawns in late fall at 40- to 49-degree water temperatures on gravel bars in stream riffles and in lakes where springs aerate eggs; female builds 4- to 12-inch-deep nest (male may guard during construction) in gravel, then buries fertilized eggs, which hatch in 50 to 150 days

Average Size: 8 to 10 inches, 8 ounces

Records: state—4 pounds, 15.2 ounces, Sunrise Lake, 1995; North American—14 pounds, 8 ounces, Nipigon River, Ontario, 1916

Notes: Introduced to Arizona in 1903, this beautiful little trout—with its voracious appetite, strong runs and delicate flavor—is prized by fishermen. Reproduces in Arizona streams but is more commonly found in lakes stocked by the Game and Fish Department. In suitable habitat it is extremely prolific; biologists have documented up to 3,500 fish per acre in some western streams.

BROWN TROUT

TIGER TROUT

Description: golden-brown to olive back and sides; large dark spots on sides, dorsal fin and sometimes upper lobe of tail; red spots with light halos scattered along sides

Similar Species: Apache Trout (pg. 106), Brook Trout (pg. 108), Rainbow Trout (pg. 116)

Brown Trout	**Apache Trout**	**Brown Trout**	**Rainbow Trout**
lacks dots on either side of pupil	dots on either side of pupil	few or no spots on slightly or non-forked tail	prominent spots on noticeably forked tail

Brown Trout	**Brook Trout**
lacks worm-like marks on back	worm-like marks on back

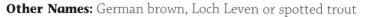
BROWN TROUT

Salmo trutta

Other Names: German brown, Loch Leven or spotted trout

Habitat: open ocean near spawning streams and clear, cold, gravel-bottomed streams; shallow areas of large reservoirs

Range: Europe from the Mediterranean to Arctic Norway and Siberia, introduced worldwide; in Arizona, streams and some lakes in the White Mountains and the Mogollon Rim

Food: insects, crayfish, small fish

Reproduction: spawns October through December in headwaters and tributaries; stream mouths are used when migration is blocked; female fans out saucer-shaped nest, deposits—and covers—up to 3,000 eggs, which male guards until spawning

Average Size: 11 to 20 inches, 2 to 6 pounds

Records: state—22 pounds, 14.5 ounces, Reservation Lake, 1999; North American—40 pounds, 4 ounces, Little Red River, Arkansas, 1992

Notes: A native of Europe, the Brown Trout was brought to North America in 1883 and Arizona in 1931. A favorite of anglers, it is a secretive, hard-to-catch fish that fights hard and has a fine, delicate flavor. Often feeds aggressively on cloudy, rainy days and at night. It tolerates warmer, cloudier water than some other trout, allowing it to live in the lower reaches of coldwater streams. Though it can survive in 80-degree F water for a short time, it prefers the 50s to lower 60s. Hybridizes with Brook Trout to produce the Tiger Trout.

111

Description: blood-red stripes on each side of throat under jaw; round, dark spots on sides and tail; breeding males develop crimson head, side and belly

Similar Species: Apache Trout (pg. 106), Brook Trout (pg. 108), Rainbow Trout (pg. 116)

Cutthroat Trout	**Brook Trout**	**Rainbow Trout**
red slash mark on throat	lacks red slash mark on throat	lacks red slash mark on throat

CUTTHROAT TROUT
Oncorhynchus clarki

Other Names: Clark's, red-throated or mountain trout, 'cutt, greenback

Habitat: clear, cold (mid-50s to low 60s F), swift-flowing, gravel-bottom headwater streams with overhanging banks or vegetation; also mountain lakes with abundant insects

Range: native to coastal streams from Alaska to California and inland waters of western North America south to the Rio Grande; in Arizona, stocked in White Mountain lakes, rare in streams

Food: freshwater shrimp, insects, small fish

Reproduction: spawns from late May to mid-July in water temperatures from 41 to 46 degrees; female excavates a 3- to 8-inch-deep, 12-inch-diameter depression in gravel bottom; a single female may lay up to 6,000 eggs; males spawn at age 2, females at age 3 or 4

Average Size: 12 inches, 1 to 2 pounds

Records: state—6 pounds, 5 ounces, Luna Lake, 1976; North American—41 pounds, Pyramid Lake, Nevada, 1925

Notes: Once thought to be a native species in Arizona, it has been concluded that early records in the Southwest were misidentified Apache or Gila Trout, or strays from the Upper Colorado drainage. Introduced to Arizona in 1900. There are numerous subspecies across western North America. Cutthroats are excellent table fare; firm, flaky fillets may be white to reddish-orange depending on the fish's diet.

113

Description: iridescent gold sides blending to dark copper on gill covers; back and sides with metallic blue sheen; head yellow with yellowish stripe on throat; dark parr marks retained in adults but fade with age; sides may have faint pink band

Similar Species: Apache Trout (pg. 106), Brown Trout (pg. 110), Roundtail Chub (pg. 62)

Gila Trout

Apache Trout

Gila Trout

Brown Trout

lacks distinct dots on either side of pupil

distinct dots on either side of pupil

small black spots and parr marks on sides

red spots on sides, lacks parr marks

Gila Trout

Apache Trout

Gila Trout

Roundtail Chub

small spots on body

large spots on body

adipose fin

lacks adipose fin

GILA TROUT
Oncorhynchus gilae

Other Names: none

Habitat: narrow, shallow, mountain headwater streams that seldom exceed 70-degree F water temperature; prefers cobble (small rock) bottom and cover such as undercut banks, logs and branches

Range: native to Upper Gila drainage in New Mexico and Verde and Agua Fria drainages in Arizona (and possibly the San Francisco drainage)

Food: aquatic and terrestrial insects, small fish

Reproduction: spawns in spring and summer, often at water temperatures of 43 to 46 degrees; beds or "redds" are constructed in 3 to 6 inches of water on fine bottom substrate; female produces average of 140 to 335 eggs, which hatch in 8 to 10 weeks (or less at warmer water temperatures)

Average Size: 5 to 11 inches

Records: none

Notes: One of two trout native to Arizona—the other being its close relative, the Apache—the Gila Trout is a rare species found in small headwater streams. Vulnerable to habitat loss from livestock grazing and logging, as well as floods, fires, drought and non-native fish, it disappeared from Arizona around 1900 and despite later stocking, was considered extirpated in 1993. Since 1999, however, recovery efforts have returned it to small streams flowing into the Blue and upper Verde river drainages.

Description: blue-green to brown head and back; silver lower sides, often with pink to rose stripe; sides, back, dorsal fins and tail are covered with small black spots

Similar Species: Apache Trout (pg. 106), Brook Trout (pg. 108), Brown Trout (pg. 110), Cutthroat Trout (pg. 112)

Rainbow Trout	**Apache Trout**	**Rainbow Trout**	**Brook Trout**
lacks dots on either side of pupil	dots on either side of pupil	lacks worm-like markings	worm-like marks on back

Rainbow Trout	**Brown Trout**	**Rainbow Trout**	**Cutthroat Trout**
prominent spots on noticeably forked tail	few or no spots on slightly or non-forked tail	lacks red slash mark on throat	red slash mark on throat

RAINBOW TROUT

Oncorhynchus mykiss

Other Names: steelhead, Pacific trout, silver trout, 'bow

Habitat: prefers whitewater in cool streams and coastal regions of large lakes, tolerates smaller cool, clear lakes

Range: Pacific Ocean and coastal streams from Mexico to Alaska and northeast Russia, introduced worldwide including the Great Lakes, southern Canada and eastern U.S.; stocked across Arizona in streams and lakes where water temperatures do not surpass 68 degrees F

Food: insects, small crustaceans, fish

Reproduction: predominantly spring spawners but some fall spawning varieties exist; female builds nest in well-aerated gravel in streams and lakes

Average Size: 8 to 20 inches, 6 ounces to 8 pounds

Records: state—15 pounds, 9.12 ounces, Willow Springs Lake, 2006; North American—42 pounds, 2 ounces, Bell Island, Alaska, 1970

Notes: This Pacific trout was first stocked in Arizona in 1898. Known for acrobatic battles and excellent table quality. Fillets are white to reddish orange depending on diet. Caught on baits ranging from worms and salmon eggs to corn, marshmallows and artificial flies and crankbaits. Reproduces in some streams and lakes but much of the state's fishery is maintained by stocking.

Description: striking iridescent appearance; sail-like dorsal fin is dusky brown to dark gray with rows of red, purple or bluish spots; dark back; grayish silver sides with dark spots; pelvic fins marked with pink to orange stripes

Similar Species: Rainbow Trout (pg. 116)

Arctic Grayling
large, sail-like dorsal fin

Rainbow Trout
small, triangular dorsal fin

ARCTIC GRAYLING

Thymallus arcticus

Other Names: grayling, sailfin

Habitat: clear, cold lakes and rivers; prefers water temperatures at or below 50 degrees F

Range: northern Canada and Alaska, with subspecies in Michigan (now extinct) and Montana; stocked elsewhere; in Arizona, high-elevation lakes in the White Mountains

Food: drifting aquatic insects such as mayflies and caddis flies, also terrestrial insects, fish eggs, crustaceans, fish

Reproduction: spawns in early spring when water temperatures reach 44 to 50 degrees; adults migrate into tributary streams or lakes or large rivers to broadcast fertilized eggs over gravel or rock bottom; no parental care

Average Size: 12 to 16 inches, 8 to 16 ounces

Records: state—1 pound, 9.76 ounces, Lee Valley Lake, 1995; North American—5 pounds, 15 ounces, Katseyedie River, Northwest Territories, 1967

Notes: This legendary fish of the Far North was introduced to Arizona in 1940 and is found in select coldwater fisheries, such as Lee Valley Reservoir and a few high-elevation lakes in the White Mountains. A willing biter on small lures, spinners and flies, it is a scrappy fighter. The male's dorsal fin is longer than the female's; he wraps it around her during spawning—ensuring as many eggs as possible are fertilized. Has excellent long-distance vision for spotting prey, but poor eyesight at close range.

Description: back and sides black to olive brown with green and copper reflections; white to pale yellow belly; sickle-shaped dorsal fin

Similar Species: Black Buffalo (pg. 122), Smallmouth Buffalo (pg. 124), Common Carp (pg. 52)

Bigmouth Buffalo

upper lip level with lower edge of eye

Black Buffalo

upper lip well below eye

Smallmouth Buffalo

upper lip well below eye

Bigmouth Buffalo

forward-facing mouth lacks barbels

Common Carp

down-turned mouth has barbels

BIGMOUTH BUFFALO

Ictiobus cyprinellus

Other Names: baldpate, gourdhead, common or redmouth buffalo

Habitat: large lakes, sloughs and oxbows; slow-flowing streams and rivers

Range: Hudson Bay, lower Great Lakes and Mississippi River basins from Ontario to Saskatchewan south to Louisiana; widely introduced; Arizona, the Salt River reservoirs and reported established in Apache and Roosevelt lakes

Food: mostly algae and crustaceans

Reproduction: migrates to spawning shoals or flooded fields and marshes in spring when water temperatures reach low 60s; scatters adhesive eggs over rocks, decomposing plants or debris; eggs hatch in 9 to 10 days at 62 degrees

Average Size: 15 to 27 inches, 2 to 14 pounds

Records: state—36 pounds, 6 ounces, Roosevelt Lake, 1995; North American—73 pounds, 1 ounce, Lake Koshkonong, Wisconsin, 2004

Notes: A non-native species introduced to Arizona in 1918, the Bigmouth Buffalo is a schooling fish typically found in the middle of the water column or near the bottom. Its large, forward-facing mouth and profusion of slender gill rakers are ideal for straining small food items such as crustaceans from the water. White, flaky meat is firm and good tasting. Seldom caught on hook and line, but may be harvested by other methods such as archery (where legal).

Description: slate-green to dark grayish blue back; sides gray to blue-bronze; deep body with sloping back; blunt snout

Similar Species: Bigmouth Buffalo (pg. 120), Common Carp (pg. 52), Smallmouth Buffalo (pg. 124)

Black Buffalo	**Bigmouth Buffalo**	**Black Buffalo**	**Smallmouth Buffalo**
upper lip well below eye	upper lip level with lower edge of eye	rounded back without hump	back steeply arched with pronounced hump

Black Buffalo	**Common Carp**
mouth lacks barbels	barbels below mouth

BLACK BUFFALO

Ictiobus niger

Other Names: blue rooter, current or mongrel buffalo

Habitat: deep, fast water of streams and rivers; reservoirs, deep backwaters and sloughs; tolerates strong current

Range: native to lower Great Lakes and Mississippi River basins from Michigan to South Dakota south to Louisiana, Texas, New Mexico and Mexico; introduced elsewhere, including the Salt River system in Arizona

Food: clams, crustaceans, algae, aquatic insects

Reproduction: spawns in spring when fish move into tributaries to deposit eggs in flooded sloughs and marshes

Average Size: 15 to 20 inches

Records: state—35 pounds, 6.72 ounces, Canyon Lake, 1995; North American—63 pounds, 6 ounces, Mississippi River, Iowa, 1999

Notes: Accidentally introduced to Arizona in 1918, the Black Buffalo is more of a bottom feeder than the Bigmouth Buffalo, prefers deeper water than the Smallmouth Buffalo, and tolerates stronger current than either one. Seldom caught on hook and line. Firm, white meat is good table fare, particularly when smoked.

Description: slate gray or green with bronze reflections; dark eye; blunt snout; small, down-turned mouth with thick lips

Similar Species: Bigmouth Buffalo (pg. 120), Common Carp (pg. 52)

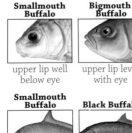

Smallmouth Buffalo — upper lip well below eye

Bigmouth Buffalo — upper lip level with eye

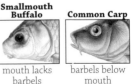

Smallmouth Buffalo — mouth lacks barbels

Common Carp — barbels below mouth

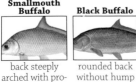

Smallmouth Buffalo — back steeply arched with pronounced hump

Black Buffalo — rounded back without hump

SMALLMOUTH BUFFALO
Ictiobus bubalus

Other Names: blue pancake, humpback or razor-backed buffalo, liner, roach-back

Habitat: moderate to fast current in deep, clear streams over sand, gravel or mixed silt bottom; less common in lakes

Range: Lake Michigan and Mississippi River basin from Pennsylvania to Montana south to Georgia, west to New Mexico into Mexico; introduced elsewhere; in Arizona, stocked in the Salt River system

Food: aquatic insects, algae, clams, crustaceans, plant debris

Reproduction: spawns in spring, in slow to medium current, when water temperatures reach the low 60s F; female deposits up to 18,000 eggs in shallow water; eggs hatch in 8 to 14 days

Average Size: 15 to 30 inches, 2 to 17 pounds

Records: state (archery)—38 pounds, 8 ounces, Canyon Lake, 1997; North American—88 pounds, Lake Wylie, North Carolina, 1993

Notes: The Smallmouth Buffalo is not native to Arizona. In some areas of its range it is commercially harvested and a highly respected food fish. Rarely caught by recreational anglers, but a strong fighter when hooked. An opportunistic feeder, it eats plant and animal matter. Found in deeper water than the Bigmouth Buffalo and lighter current than the Black Buffalo.

BLUEHEAD SUCKER

ZUNI BLUEHEAD SUCKER

Description: dark back; grayish-blue to tan or yellowish
sides; head of adults often develops bluish color; long,
slender body

Similar Species: Desert Sucker (pg. 128), Zuni Bluehead
Sucker

Bluehead Sucker	**Desert Sucker**	**Zuni Bluehead Sucker**
bluish head; body length 10 to 20 inches	lacks blue on head	lacks blue on head; body less than 8 inches

BLUEHEAD SUCKER

Catostomus (Pantosteus) discobolus

Other Names: bluehead mountain sucker

Habitat: middle and upper Colorado River drainage Arizona, Colorado, New Mexico, Utah and Wyoming; in Arizona, the Colorado mainstem and Grand Canyon tributaries; rare below Diamond Creek, but possible in other areas

Range: headwater streams to large rivers with medium to strong current and rocky bottoms; found in cold, clear streams and warm, turbid (cloudy) rivers

Food: algae, invertebrates

Reproduction: spawns in spring and summer when water temperatures surpass 60 degrees F; 2 to 5 males join female, deposit fertilized eggs over gravel, sand and small rocks

Average Size: 10 to 20 inches

Records: state—none; North American—2 pounds, 9 ounces, Strawberry River, Utah, 1992

Notes: A creature of the current, the Bluehead Sucker requires medium to strong flows. In rivers or streams with predominantly sand bottoms, look for it around rocky shoals. Its mouth is lined with ridges of hard cartilage used to scrape algae and invertebrates off rocks. Blueheads in fast streams have a thin caudal peduncle (connection from body to tail); those in slower water are thicker-bodied. Subspecies Zuni Bluehead Sucker (*Catostomus discobolus yarrowi*) is found in headwaters of the Little Colorado River. It is usually less than 8 inches in length.

127

Description: distinctly bi-colored body is silver-tan to dark greenish brown above, silvery to deep yellow below; large lips with cartilage edge inside; usually 10 or 11 dorsal rays

Similar Species: Sonora Sucker (pg. 136)

Desert Sucker	Sonora Sucker
cartilage ridge inside lips	lacks cartilage ridge inside lips

DESERT SUCKER

Catostomus (Pantosteus) clarki

Other Names: Gila mountain sucker

Habitat: rivers and streams with deep, quiet pools with rock or gravel bottom; does not tolerate reservoir conditions

Range: tributaries of the Gila River drainage above Gila, Arizona, the lower Colorado River below the Grand Canyon, and the Virgin River basin of Arizona, Nevada and Utah; in Arizona, currently common but locally declining in the Bill Williams, Gila, Salt and Verde river systems

Food: aquatic insect larvae, algae

Reproduction: spawns February to early July on gravel bottom in riffles; a large female, attended by several smaller males, deposits adhesive eggs in shallow depression in gravel; eggs hatch within a few days with no parental care

Average Size: 8 to 31 inches, 4 ounces to 4 pounds

Records: state and North American—2 pounds, 10.75 ounces, Verde River, 1992

Notes: The Desert Sucker is an Arizona native. Considered a sportfish, it can be caught on live bait such as worms or crickets fished on the bottoms of deep pools. Firm, white meat has a good flavor; intermuscular or "floating" bones may be removed before cooking. Adult Desert Suckers typically hold in pools by day, and move into riffles and runs to feed under the cover of darkness. They feed by scraping cartilage-sheathed jaws on stones and may turn belly up to scour the underside of food-rich underwater objects.

Description: greenish-blue to gray back; yellowish sides; white belly; when taken from cloudy water, may have tan back, white to silver sides and belly; blunt snout

Similar Species: Little Colorado Sucker (pg. 132)

Flannelmouth Sucker	Little Colorado Sucker
thin caudal peduncle (area connecting tail to body)	thick caudal peduncle (area connecting tail to body)

FLANNELMOUTH SUCKER

Catostomus latipinnis

Other Names: none

Habitat: large rivers and streams; found in varied habitat, including deep pools, riffles, runs, eddies and backwater areas; not usually found in reservoirs

Range: Colorado River drainage; in Arizona, the Colorado River and its larger tributaries in Glen and Grand canyons, including the Virgin River

Food: algae and other plant matter, aquatic invertebrates

Reproduction: spawns in streams in spring over gravel bottom

Average Size: 12 to 24 inches, 2 to 3 pounds

Records: state—none; North American—4 pounds, 5 ounces, Flaming Gorge Reservoir, Utah, 1992

Notes: Its streamlined body makes the Flannelmouth Sucker well suited to the turbulent waters of the Colorado River drainage. Though it can be found in a variety of riverine habitats, from deep pools with slow flows to riffles and backwaters, it doesn't do well in reservoir situations. Throughout its range, the Flannelmouth appears to fare poorly from competition with the arrival of non-native suckers. Cold water released from reservoirs could also play a role in their decline in some tailwater areas.

Description: dark gray to bluish black back; white to yellow sides and belly; large scales; large head and chubby, bi-colored body

Similar Species: Flannelmouth Sucker (pg. 130)

Little Colorado Sucker

thick caudal peduncle (area connecting tail to body)

Flannelmouth Sucker

thin caudal peduncle (area connecting tail to body)

LITTLE COLORADO SUCKER

Catostomus sp. 3

Other Names: Little Colorado River Sucker

Habitat: creeks, small to medium-size rivers and impoundments; commonly found in pools with ample cover, but will also hold in riffles

Range: upper sections of the Little Colorado River and north-flowing tributaries in Apache, Coconino and Navajo counties

Food: algae and other plant matter, aquatic invertebrates and detritus

Reproduction: spawns in early to mid-spring; young fish favor slow-flowing riffles

Average Size: up to 19.7 inches, 2 pounds

Records: none

Notes: Naturally separated from the rest of the Colorado River system by a series of falls, the Little Colorado Sucker is an interesting native species that is very similar to the Flannelmouth Sucker. It feeds late in the evening and early morning, when large adults move into riffle areas and stir up large areas of gravel and sand while searching for food. Its populations have declined due to habitat loss—mainly reduction in stream flows, water diversions, erosion, dams and the introduction of non-native fish species.

Description: bronze to brownish green back and sides; yellowish to white belly; bony, keel-like hump on back; breeding males turn gray-black with orange belly

Similar Species: Humpback Chub (pg. 60)

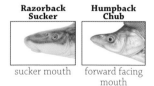

Razorback Sucker	Humpback Chub
sucker mouth	forward facing mouth

RAZORBACK SUCKER

Xyrauchen texanus

Other Names: buffalo, buffalofish, humpback sucker

Habitat: deep, clear to turbid (cloudy) large rivers and reservoirs; often associated with mud, sand or gravel bottom; often reported in quiet, soft-bottom backwaters; tolerates water to nearly 90 degrees F but prefers 71 to 77 degrees

Range: Colorado and Gila basins from Wyoming to Mexico; in Arizona, native to Colorado, Gila, Salt, Verde and San Pedro rivers; currently, lakes Havasu, Mead and Mohave

Food: algae, insect larvae, bottom debris, plankton

Reproduction: matures at 3 to 4 years; spawns late winter into spring in tributaries along gravel shorelines and in bays; up to 12 males attend lone female; adhesive eggs attach to gravel and hatch within several days; water temperatures below 50 degrees are fatal to eggs

Average Size: up to 36 inches, 8 to 13 pounds

Records: state—9 pounds, 13 ounces, Lake Havasu, 1978; North American—6 pounds, 4 ounces, Colorado River, Nevada, 1977

Notes: Once so abundant that farmers ground it into feed and fertilizer, the Razorback Sucker is an amazing native Arizona species. One of North America's largest suckers, it can reach more than 3 feet in length and weights of 12 to 14 pounds; reported to live more than 40 years in Lake Mohave. Dams, pollution, the arrival of non-native competitors and predators all took a toll on this unique fish.

135

Description: distinctly bi-colored body is brownish above, yellow below; dark spots on upper body scales form "dash lines"; large head

Similar Species: Common Carp, (pg. 52), Desert Sucker (pg. 128), Flannelmouth Sucker (pg. 130)

Sonora Sucker	Common Carp
distinct sucker mouth lacks barbels	down-turned mouth has barbels

Sonora Sucker	Desert Sucker
usually fewer than 60 lateral line scales	61 to 104 lateral line scales

Sonora Sucker	Flannelmouth Sucker
spots on scales form dash lines	sides lack dash lines

SONORA SUCKER

Catostomus insignis

Other Names: Gila Sucker

Habitat: tolerates diverse habitats from trout streams to warmwater rivers; prefers rocky or gravel-bottom pools; primarily a stream fish but some lake populations reported

Range: Colorado River basin of Arizona and New Mexico; northern Sonora, Mexico; in Arizona, widespread in Gila and Bill Williams drainages, rare to absent in Salt River Canyon

Food: algae, diatoms, aquatic insects

Reproduction: spawns late winter through midsummer in riffles; typically attended by two males, female deposits eggs over gravel; eggs settle into small openings; spawns mostly in streams, but some lake spawning reported

Average Size: up to 31 inches and more than 4 pounds

Records: state—5 pounds, 6.4 ounces, Canal Park Lake, 1996; North American—none

Notes: Native to Arizona, the Sonora Sucker is largely a stream fish but some individuals have been collected in Roosevelt Lake. An opportunistic feeder, it will eat a variety of foods ranging from insect larvae to plant debris on the bottom, and has even been observed sipping tree seeds off the surface. Massive schools of young Sonora Suckers school along shorelines to dine upon tiny crustaceans and other microscopic food items. Reaches weight of more than 4 pounds and will take a hook tipped with live bait; the fillets are white, firm and good-tasting.

Description: dark green back, greenish sides often with dark lateral band; belly white to gray; large, forward-facing mouth; lower jaw extends to rear margin of eye

Similar Species: Smallmouth Bass (pg. 140)

Largemouth Bass
Smallmouth Bass

mouth extends well beyond non-red eye

mouth does not extend beyond red eye

LARGEMOUTH BASS

Centrarchidae

Micropterus salmoides

Other Names: green bass, green trout, slough bass

Habitat: shallow, fertile, weedy lakes and river backwaters; weedy bays and weedbeds of large lakes; deep structure and flooded timber in clear, well-oxygenated reservoirs

Range: southern Canada through U.S. into Mexico, widely introduced; in Arizona, found in the Colorado, Gila, lower Salt and lower Verde rivers and associated reservoirs

Food: small fish, frogs, crayfish, insects, leeches

Reproduction: matures at 3 to 5 years; spawns March through June when water reaches 60 degrees F; male builds nest on firm bottom in weedy cover; female deposits up to 40,000 eggs, which male fans and guards; eggs hatch in about 3 to 4 days; male protects fry until the "brood swarm" disperses

Average Size: 12 to 20 inches, 1 to 5 pounds

Records: state—16 pounds, 7.68 ounces, Canyon Lake, 1997; North American—22 pounds, 4 ounces, Montgomery Lake, Georgia, 1932

Notes: A non-native that is prized by anglers, the Largemouth Bass arrived in Arizona in 1897. It is an aggressive predator from the time it begins feeding 5 to 8 days after hatching. Young bass eat tiny creatures such as copepods, waterfleas and insect larvae. Before the end of the first growing season, fish are added to the menu.

139

Description: back and sides mottled dark green to bronze or pale gold, often with dark vertical bands; white belly; stout body; large, forward-facing mouth; red eye

Similar Species: Largemouth Bass (pg. 138)

Smallmouth Bass **Largemouth Bass**

mouth does not extend beyond red eye

mouth extends well beyond non-red eye

SMALLMOUTH BASS

Micropterus dolomieu

Other Names: bronzeback, brown or redeye bass, redeye, white or mountain trout

Habitat: clear, cool streams and rivers with near-permanent flow; clear lakes with gravel or rocky shores, bars and reefs

Range: extensively introduced throughout North America; abundant in the Black and Verde rivers and Apache Lake in Arizona, also found in lakes Roosevelt and Powell

Food: small fish, crayfish, insects, frogs

Reproduction: matures at 4 years; spawns March into May, when water reaches mid- to high 60s F; in streams, male fans out nest in backwater on gravel; lake nests are often next to a log or boulder; female lays up to 14,000 eggs, which hatch in about 2 to 7 days; male guards nest and fry

Average Size: 12 to 20 inches, 1 to 4 pounds

Records: state—7 pounds, 0.96 ounces, Roosevelt Lake, 1988; North American—11 pounds, 15 ounces; Dale Hollow Lake, Tennessee, 1955

Notes: An introduced species that came to Arizona in 1921, the Smallmouth Bass is a world-class game fish noted for powerful fights and wild jumps. Avoiding weedbeds, it prefers deeper, more open water than the Largemouth Bass. In streams, it is often found over silt-free rock or gravel near riffles around rootwads, large rocks and other cover—but not in the main current. In lakes, it favors riprap shores and rocky structure offshore.

Description: black to dark olive back with purple to emerald reflections; silver sides with dark green or black blotches; back slightly more arched—and depression above eye less pronounced—than White Crappie

Similar Species: White Crappie (pg. 144)

Black Crappie	White Crappie	Black Crappie	White Crappie
usually 7 to 8 spines in dorsal fin	usually 5 to 6 spines in dorsal fin	dorsal fin length equal to distance from dorsal to eye	dorsal fin shorter than distance from eye to dorsal

142

BLACK CRAPPIE
Pomoxis nigromaculatus

Other Names: papermouth, speck, speckled perch, calico bass

Habitat: quiet, clear water of streams and mid-sized lakes; often associated with weeds or flooded timber and brush, but may roam deep, open basins and flats

Range: native to southern Manitoba through the Atlantic and southeastern states, introduced in the West; common in most large warmwater reservoirs in Arizona

Food: small fish, aquatic insects, zooplankton

Reproduction: matures at 2 to 3 years; spawns in colonies in spring and early summer when water reaches high 50s F; male sweeps out circular nest, typically on silt-free bottom of fine gravel or sand (sometimes mud)—often next to a plant, log or other object; female may produce more than 180,000 eggs, which hatch in about 3 to 5 days; male guards nest and fry until young are feeding on their own

Average Size: 7 to 12 inches, 10 ounces to 1 pound

Records: state—4 pounds, 10 ounces, San Carlos Lake, 1959; North American—6 pounds, Westwego Canal, Louisiana, 1969

Notes: Introduced to Arizona in 1905, the Black Crappie is pursued year-round by anglers for its sweet-tasting, white fillets. It is an aggressive carnivore that will hit everything from live minnows to jigging spoons and small crankbaits. Adults feed heavily on other fish—Threadfin Shad are a main food item in Arizona. Though not noted for its fighting ability, the Black Crappie puts up a good struggle on light tackle.

143

Description: greenish to dark olive back with purple to emerald reflections; silvery green to white sides with 7 to 9 dark,
vertical bars; anal fin almost as large as dorsal

Similar Species: Black Crappie (pg. 142)

White Crappie

usually 5 to 6
spines in
dorsal fin

Black Crappie

usually 7 to 8
spines in
dorsal fin

White Crappie

dorsal fin
shorter than
distance from
eye to dorsal

Black Crappie

dorsal fin
length equal to
distance from
dorsal to eye

WHITE CRAPPIE

Pomoxis annularis

Other Names: silver, pale or ringed crappie, papermouth

Habitat: slightly silty streams and mid-size lakes; more tolerant of warm, turbid (cloudy) conditions than Black Crappie

Range: North Dakota south and east to the Gulf and Atlantic except peninsular Florida, introduced elsewhere; Lake Pleasant is the only regular producer of the species in Arizona

Food: aquatic insects, small fish, plankton

Reproduction: matures at 2 to 3 years; spawns on firm sand or gravel bottom in spring and early summer when water temp approaches 60 degrees F; male fans out nest, often near a log or plant roots; female deposits 3,000 to 15,000 eggs, which hatch in 3 to 5 days; male guards eggs and fry

Average Size: 6 to 12 inches, 8 ounces to 1 pound

Records: state—3 pounds, 5.28 ounces, Lake Pleasant, 1982; North American—5 pounds, 3 ounces, Enid Dam, Mississippi, 1957

Notes: A non-native introduced to Arizona in 1903, the White Crappie is popular with anglers thanks to its flavorful white fillets. It is often found in large but relatively loose schools, suspended off bottom and away from weeds and structure. In reservoirs where flooded timber is available, however, it may relate to this woody cover. Actively feeds at night and during the winter. Due to its tolerance of turbid (cloudy) water, there is some indication of a positive relationship between the White Crappie and Common Carp.

145

Description: dark olive to green back, blending to silver-gray, copper, orange, purple or brown on sides with 5 to 9 dark, vertical bars that may fade with age; yellow underside and copper breast; dark gill spot; dark spot on rear of dorsal fin

Similar Species: Green Sunfish (pg. 148), Redear Sunfish (pg. 150), Warmouth (pg. 154)

Bluegill	**Green Sunfish**	**Warmouth**
mouth does not extend to eye	large mouth extends to eye	jaw extends to middle of eye

Bluegill	**Redear Sunfish**
dark ear flap	red or orange on ear flap

BLUEGILL

Lepomis macrochirus

Other Names: bream, copperbelly, pond perch

Habitat: reservoirs and ponds, particularly those with weedy bays or shorelines; also found in oxbows of streams, and occasionally in mainstem areas below current breaks

Range: southern Canada into Mexico; common across Arizona in suitable habitat below 4,000 feet in elevation

Food: insects, small fish, leeches, snails, zooplankton, algae

Reproduction: typically matures by second summer; spawns from April into summer in water from 67 to 80 degrees F; "parental" male excavates nest in gravel or sand, often in weeds, in colony of up to 50 other nests; smaller "cuckholder" male (exhibiting female behavior and coloration) may dart in and fertilize eggs; after spawning, parental male chases female away and guards nest until fry disperse

Average Size: 6 to 9$\frac{1}{2}$ inches, 5 to 12 ounces

Records: state—3 pounds, 15.68 ounces, Goldwater Lake, 2004; North American—4 pounds, 12 ounces; Ketona Lake, Alabama, 1950

Notes: Introduced to Arizona in 1932, it is a favorite of anglers for its tenacious fight and excellent table quality. Small fish are easy to catch near docks in summer. Larger "bulls" favor deeper water, often near cliffs, weedlines and other cover much of the year. During the spawn, colonies are targeted and sometimes overfished. Hybridizes with other sunfish. Acute daytime vision but sees poorly in low light.

Description: dark green back; dark olive to bluish sides; yellow or whitish belly; scales flecked with yellow, producing a brassy appearance; dark gill spot has a pale margin

Similar Species: Bluegill (pg. 146)

Green Sunfish

mouth extends
to eye

Bluegill

mouth does not
extend to eye

GREEN SUNFISH

Lepomis cyanellus

Centrarchidae

Other Names: black perch, blue-spotted sunfish, sand bass

Habitat: warmwater lakes with cover such as weeds or brush, or rock-rubble bottoms; also found in the backwaters of slow-moving streams and some coolwater trout fisheries

Range: most of the U.S. into Mexico except Florida and the Rocky Mountains; in Arizona, found in most warmwater lakes and streams, and some trout lakes

Food: aquatic and terrestrial insects, crustaceans, small fish

Reproduction: spawns in water from 60 to 80 degrees F and can produce two broods per season; male fans out nest on gravel bottom in shallow water, near cover—often beneath overhanging limbs; male may grunt to lure female into nest; after spawning, male guards nest and fans eggs

Average Size: 5 to 8 inches, less than 12 ounces

Records: state—1 pound, 9 ounces, Parker Canyon Lake, 1996; North American—2 pounds, 2 ounces, Stockton Lake, Missouri, 1971

Notes: Introduced in 1926, it is easy to catch but not a popular sportfish because it rarely reaches more than 5 to 7 inches in length. It is highly prolific and may overpopulate a lake with stunted, 3-inch bait robbers. Tolerant of high siltation and low oxygen levels, it thrives in warm, weedy lakes and backwaters. Also withstands drought conditions and is often among the last survivors in the pools of intermittent streams. Hybridizes with Bluegill and other sunfish.

149

Description: bronze to dark green back and sides, fading to light green with faint vertical bars; short gill spot is tinged red on males; blue stripes on head

Similar Species: Bluegill (pg. 146)

Redear Sunfish

red crescent on gill flap

Bluegill

lacks red on gill flap

REDEAR SUNFISH

Lepomis microlophus

Other Names: shellcracker, stumpknocker, yellow bream

Habitat: prefers clear, quiet lakes with some weedgrowth; seldom found in current; often relates to woody cover such as submerged stumps or logs, also deep bottom structure

Range: Midwest through southern states; introduced in the West and some northern states; in Arizona, statewide in warmwater lakes and ponds

Food: clams, snails, insect larvae

Reproduction: matures at end of second year; spawns in shallow water—though typically slightly deeper than other sunfish—late spring and early summer; male builds saucer-shaped bed in gravel or silt bottom

Average Size: 8 to 11 inches, 1 pound

Records: 3 pounds, 9 ounces, Goldwater Lake, 1993; North American—5 pounds, 7.5 ounces, Diversion Canal, South Carolina, 1998

Notes: Beloved by anglers for its large size and tasty white fillets, the Redear Sunfish is a southern species introduced in the Southwest and elsewhere. It arrived in Arizona in 1946 and is now found statewide in suitable warmwater habitat. It rarely takes baits off the surface but will hit worms and grubs, especially fished on or near bottom.

151

Description: brown to olive green back and sides with dark spots and overall bronze appearance; red eye; thicker, heavier body than other sunfish; large mouth

Similar Species: Bluegill (pg. 146), Green Sunfish (pg. 148), Warmouth (pg. 154)

Rock Bass / **Bluegill**

mouth extends to eye / mouth does not extend to eye

Rock Bass / **Warmouth**

lacks red-brown streaks radiating from eye / 3 to 5 red-brown streaks radiate from eye

Rock Bass / **Green Sunfish**

6 spines in anal fin / 3 spines in anal fin

ROCK BASS

Ambloplites rupestris

Other Names: redeye, goggle-eye, rock sunfish

Habitat: vegetation on firm to rocky bottom in clear-water lakes and medium-size streams

Range: southern Canada through central and eastern U.S. to northern edge of Gulf states; in Arizona, introduced in lakes above the Mogollon Rim, the upper Verde system and lowermost Clear Creek in the Little Colorado drainage

Food: prefers crayfish, but eats aquatic insects and small fish

Reproduction: matures at 2 to 3 years; spawns in spring at water temperatures from high 60s to 70s F; male fans out 8- to 10-inch-diameter nest in 1 to 5 feet of water, on coarse sand or gravel bottom, often next to a boulder or in weeds; male guards eggs and fry

Average Size: 8 to 10 inches, 8 ounces to 1 pound

Records: state—12.96 ounces, Upper Verde River, 2006; North American—3 pounds, York River, Ontario, 1974

Notes: A non-native species, the chunky Rock Bass is a secretive fish that frequents weedbeds associated with rocky, sandy or gravel bottoms. It has the chameleon-like ability to change colors to match its surroundings. Though the Rock Bass is hard-fighting and good tasting, it is seldom targeted by anglers. It may feed anytime during the day, but is most active at dusk and during the night.

Description: back and sides greenish gray to brown; lightly mottled with faint vertical bands; stout body; large mouth; red eye; 3 to 5 reddish-brown streaks radiate from eye

Similar Species: Bluegill (pg. 146), Green Sunfish (pg. 148), Rock Bass (pg. 152)

Warmouth	**Bluegill**		**Warmouth**	**Green Sunfish**

 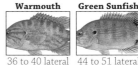

jaw extends to middle of eye	jaw does not extend to eye		36 to 40 lateral scales	44 to 51 lateral scales

Warmouth	**Rock Bass**

3 to 5 red-brown streaks radiate from eye	lacks red-brown streaks radiating from eye

WARMOUTH
Lepomis gulosus

Other Names: goggle-eye, stumpknocker, weed bass

Habitat: heavy weeds or flooded woody cover in natural lakes, reservoirs and slow-moving streams; prefers clear water and mud bottom

Range: southern U.S. from Texas to Florida north to the Great Lakes region; in Arizona, introduced into the lower Colorado River system and reservoirs on the Salt River

Food: small fish, insects, snails, crustaceans

Reproduction: spawns in May and June, when water temps reach the low 70s F; not a colonial nester like other sunfish; male fans out bed in dense, shallow weeds, often near a rock, stump or thick weed clump; male guards eggs

Average Size: 11 inches, 8 to 12 ounces

Records: state (Colorado River waters)—12 ounces, Senator Wash Reservoir, 1974; North American—2 pounds, 7 ounces, Yellow River, Florida, 1985

Notes: This secretive sunfish is a solitary, aggressive sight-feeder that, when not hiding in dense vegetation, is often found around rocks and submerged stumps. It withstands low oxygen levels, high silt loads and water temperatures well into the 90s. While nest guarding, the male drives off intruders by flaring its gills and opening its mouth, while its eyes turn blood red and its body takes on a bright yellow coloration. Its small size keeps it off the radar of most anglers, but it has a good flavor and is a good fighter.

Description: bluish to dark olive-green back; silver on sides with about 7 dark, horizontal streaks; white belly; base of tongue has two parallel patches of teeth; usually 11 to 12 soft rays in second dorsal fin; body depth less than one-third length to base of tail (as opposed to deeper-bodied White Bass); two spines on gill cover

Similar Species: White Bass (pg. 158), Yellow Bass (pg. 160)

Striped Bass	**White Bass**	**Striped Bass**	**Yellow Bass**
two spines on gill cover	single spine on gill cover	horizontal stripes unbroken	horizontal stripes broken above anal fin

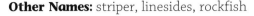

STRIPED BASS

Morone saxatilis

Moronidae

Other Names: striper, linesides, rockfish

Habitat: fresh- or saltwater; schools roam clear water along shorelines and bays, but are also found in open water

Range: native to East Coast of North America from lower St. Lawrence River to northern Florida and parts of the Gulf of Mexico; widely introduced; in Arizona, the Colorado River from Lake Powell to the Mexican border, also Lake Pleasant

Food: small fish (such as Threadfin Shad), insects, crustaceans

Reproduction: matures from age 2 (males) to 3 or 4 (females); migrates into rivers and to reservoir shoals, headwaters or tailwaters below a dam in spring or early summer, in water from 60 to 68 degrees F; spawns in moving water; successful reproduction requires constant current because the semi-buoyant eggs must remain off the bottom and have plenty of oxygen until hatching—usually in 36 to 75 hours

Average Size: 22 to 36 inches, 5 to 20 pounds

Records: state—27 pounds, 4.48 ounces, Lake Pleasant, 2007; North American—67 pounds, 1 ounce, Colorado River, Arizona, 1997 (also Arizona state record for fish taken from Colorado River waters)

Notes: This schooling, open-water fish came to Arizona in 1959. Highly adaptable, it can survive in saltwater, freshwater and brackish conditions in water temperatures up to about 95 degrees. Given ample forage, it can reach nearly 30 inches in length and 10 pounds in 5 growing seasons.

157

Description: bright silver; 6 to 8 distinct, uninterrupted black stripes on each side; front hard-spined portion of dorsal fin separated from soft-rayed rear section; lower jaw protrudes beyond snout

Similar Species: Striped Bass (pg. 156), Yellow Bass (pg. 160)

White Bass

lower jaw protrudes beyond snout

Yellow Bass

lower jaw even with snout

White Bass

single spine on gill cover

Striped Bass

two spines on gill cover

White Bass

single tooth patch on tongue

Striped Bass

two tooth patches

Yellow Bass

no teeth on tongue

WHITE BASS
Morone chrysops

Other Names: silver bass, streaker, lake bass, sand bass

Habitat: large lakes and rivers with relatively clear water

Range: Great Lakes region to the eastern seaboard, through the southeast to the Gulf, introduced elsewhere; in Arizona, found in Imperial Reservoir on the Colorado River and in Lake Pleasant

Food: small fish (such as Threadfin Shad), insects, crustaceans

Reproduction: spawns in April and May at water temperatures of 55 to 79 degrees F, in open water over gravel beds or rubble 6 to 10 feet deep; a single female may produce more than 500,000 eggs

Average Size: 9 to 18 inches, 8 ounces to 2 pounds

Records: state—4 pounds, 11.7 ounces, Upper Lake Pleasant, 1972; North American—6 pounds, 7 ounces, Saginaw Bay, Michigan, 1989

Notes: Introduced to Arizona in 1960, the White Bass is a willing striker and hard fighter that favors deep pools in streams and open water in large lakes. It travels and hunts in large schools that are often spotted near the surface; watch for seagulls feeding on "boils" of frightened baitfish that flee these marauding predators. White Bass fillets are of good table quality; like most species, the flavor and texture can be preserved if the fish are quickly put on ice.

159

Description: silvery yellow to brassy sides with yellowish white belly; 6 or 7 black stripes, broken above the anal fin; forked tail; two sections of dorsal connected by membrane

Similar Species: Striped Bass (pg. 156), White Bass (pg. 158)

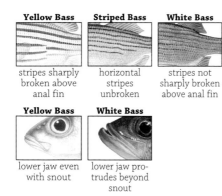

Yellow Bass	**Striped Bass**	**White Bass**
stripes sharply broken above anal fin	horizontal stripes unbroken	stripes not sharply broken above anal fin

Yellow Bass	**White Bass**
lower jaw even with snout	lower jaw protrudes beyond snout

YELLOW BASS

Morone mississippiensis

Other Names: brassy or gold bass, barfish

Habitat: open water over shallow gravel bars

Range: Mississippi River drainage from Minnesota to Gulf of Mexico, introduced elsewhere; in Arizona, the Salt River reservoirs—Apache, Canyon and Saguaro—and Lake Mary

Food: small fish, insects, crustaceans

Reproduction: spawns in late spring, in or at the mouths of tributary streams, over gravel bars in 2 to 3 feet of water; eggs hatch in 4 to 6 days at 70 degrees

Average Size: 8 to 12 inches, 8 to 16 ounces

Records: state— 1 pound, 15.8 ounces, Upper Lake Mary, 1995; North American—2 pounds, 8 ounces, Tennessee River, Alabama, 2000

Notes: The Yellow Bass is similar in behavior and biology to its slightly larger cousin, the White Bass. A schooling fish, it tends to relate a bit more to structure than the White Bass, and often is found in the middle to lower sections of the water column. A non-native species, it was introduced to Arizona waters in 1930. A population in Roosevelt Lake failed but it persists in the waters mentioned above. In some areas of its range, the Yellow Bass is a popular pan-fish with anglers who consider its flaky, white fillets superior to those of White Bass.

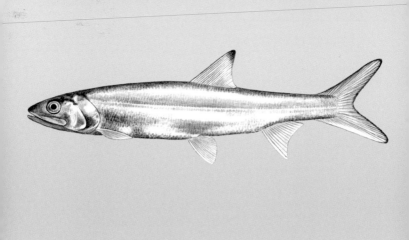

Description: overall silver coloration, with yellowish tinge in eyes and the bases of paired fins; dorsal and anal fins fit into sheaths of scales at base; elongated body; straight lateral line

Similar Species: Striped Mullet (pg. 96)

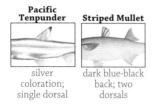

Pacific Tenpunder
silver coloration; single dorsal

Striped Mullet
dark blue-black back; two dorsals

PACIFIC TENPOUNDER

Elopidae

Elops affinis

Other Names: ladyfish, machete

Habitat: coastal inshore areas, prefers depths up to 26 feet; moves into estuaries, lagoons and freshwater rivers to feed

Range: eastern Pacific from Peru to California, including the Colorado River delta in the Gulf of California; in Arizona, occurs sporadically in the Lower Colorado River

Food: fish, crustaceans

Reproduction: spawns in the open ocean; planktonic eggs are broadcast far offshore; near-transparent larvae (distinguished from eels by forked tail) migrate toward coastlines, where they feed and develop in fresh- and brackish water

Average Size: up to 3 feet and 9 pounds in the Pacific; to 14 inches in the Colorado River

Records: state—12.6 ounces, near Pilot Knob, 1981

Notes: The Pacific Tenpounder is primarily a saltwater fish that moves into brackish (slightly salty) or freshwater. Common in Colorado River delta in the Gulf of California and formerly abundant in California's Salton Sea. Because juveniles move into freshwater rivers to feed, often after floods, the average size of river-run Tenpounders is less than that of those found at sea. Puts up a strong fight on light tackle.

GLOSSARY

adipose fin a small, fleshy fin without rays, located on the midline of the fish's back between the dorsal fin and the tail

air bladder a balloon-like organ located in the gut area of a fish, used to control buoyancy—and in the respiration of some species such as gar; also called "swim bladder" or "gas bladder"

alevin a newly hatched fish that still has its yolk sac

anadromous a fish that hatches in freshwater, migrates to the ocean, then re-enters streams or rivers from the sea (or large inland body of water) to spawn

anal fin a single fin located on the bottom of the fish near the tail

annulus marks or rings on the scales, spine, vertebrae or otoliths that scientists use to determine a fish's age

anterior toward the front of a fish, opposite of posterior

bands horizontal marks running lengthwise along the side of a fish

barbel thread-like sensory structures on a fish's head often near the mouth, commonly called "whiskers;" used for taste or smell

bars vertical markings on the side of a fish

benthic organisms living in or on the bottom

brood swarm large group of young fish such as bullheads

cardiform teeth small teeth on the lips of a catfish

carnivore a fish that feeds on other fish or animals

catadromous a fish that lives in freshwater and migrates into saltwater to spawn, such as the American Eel

caudal fin tail fin

caudal peduncle the portion of the fish's body located between the anal fin and the beginning of the tail

ciénegas small, shallow wetlands in the Southwest, fed by springs or geologic formations forcing groundwater to the surface; critical habitat for some native fishes

coldwater referring to a species or environment; in fish, often a species of trout or salmon found in water that rarely exceeds 70 degrees F; also used to describe a lake or river according to average summer temperature

copepod a small (less than 2 mm) crustacean that is part of the zooplankton community

crustacean a crayfish, water flea, crab or other animal belonging to group of mostly aquatic species that have paired antennae, jointed legs and an exterior skeleton (exoskeleton); common food for many fish

dorsal relating to the top of the fish, on or near the back; opposite of the ventral, or lower, part of the fish

dorsal fin the fin or fins located along the top of a fish's back

eddy a circular water current, often created by an obstruction

epilimnion the warm, oxygen-rich upper layer of water in a thermally stratified lake

exotic a foreign species, not native to a watershed

extirpated eliminated from a geographic area, often a species' native range

fingerling a juvenile fish, generally 1 to 10 inches in length, in its first year of life

fork length the overall length of a fish from the mouth to the deepest part of the tail notch

fry recently hatched young fish that have absorbed their yolk sacs

game fish a species regulated by laws for recreational fishing

gills organs used in aquatic respiration

gill cover large bone covering the gills, also called opercle or operculum

gill raker a comblike projection from the gill arch

harvest fish that are caught and kept by sport or commercial anglers

hypolimnion bottom layer of water in a thermally stratified lake (common in summer), usually depleted of oxygen by decaying matter

ichthyologist a scientist who studies fish

invertebrates animals without backbones, such as insects, crayfish, leeches and earthworms

lateral line a series of pored scales along the side of a fish that contain organs used to detect vibrations

littoral zone the part of a lake that is less than 15 feet in depth; this important and often vulnerable area holds the majority of aquatic plants, is a primary area used by young fish, and offers essential spawning habitat for most warmwater fishes such as Walleye and Largemouth Bass

mandible lower jaw

maxillary upper jaw

milt semen of a male fish that fertilizes the female's eggs during spawning

mollusk an invertebrate with a smooth, soft body such as a clam or a snail

native an indigenous or naturally occurring species

omnivore a fish or animal that eats plants and animal matter

otolith an L-shaped bone found in the inner ear of fish

opercle bone covering the gills, also called gill cover or operculum

panfish small freshwater game fish that can be fried whole in a pan, such as crappies, perch and sunfish

pectoral fins paired fins on the side of the fish just behind the gills

pelagic fish species that live in open water, in the food-rich upper layer of water; not associated with the bottom

pelvic fins paired fins below or behind the pectoral fins on the bottom (ventral portion) of the fish

pharyngeal teeth tooth-like structures in the throat on the margins of the gill bars

pheromone a chemical scent secreted as a means of communication between members of the same species

piscivore a predatory fish that mainly eats other fish

planktivore a fish that feeds on plankton

plankton floating or weakly swimming aquatic plants and animals, including larval fish, that drift with the current; often eaten by fish; individual organisms are called plankters

plankton bloom a marked increase in the amount of plankton due to favorable conditions such as nutrients and light

range the geographic region in which a species is found

ray hard supporting part of the fin; resembles a spine but is jointed (can be raised and lowered) and is barbed; found in catfish, carp and goldfish

ray soft flexible structures supporting the fin membrane, sometimes branched

redd a nest-like depression made by a male or female fish during the spawn, often refers to nest of trout and salmon species

riparian area land adjacent to streams, rivers, lakes and other wetlands where the vegetation is influenced by the great availability of water

riprap rock or concrete used to protect a lake shore or river bank from erosion

roe fish eggs

scales small, flat plates covering the outer skin of many fish

Secchi disk a black-and-white circular disk used to measure water clarity; scientists record the average depth at which the disk disappears from sight when lowered into the water

silt small, easily disturbed bottom particles smaller than sand but larger than clay

siltation the accumulation of soil particles

spawning the process of fish reproduction; involves females laying eggs and males fertilizing them to produce young fish

spine stiff, pointed structures found along with soft rays in some fins; unlike hard rays they are not jointed

spiracle an opening on the posterior portion of the head above and behind the eye

standard length length of the fish from the mouth to the end of the vertebral column

stocking the purposeful, artificial introduction of a fish species into an area

substrate bottom composition of a lake, stream or river

subterminal mouth below the snout of the fish

swim bladder see air bladder

tailrace area immediately downstream of a dam or power plant

tapetum lucidum reflective pigment in a Walleye's eye

thermocline middle layer of water in a stratified lake, typically oxygen rich, characterized by a sharp drop in water temperature; often the lowest depth at which fish can be routinely found

terminal mouth forward facing

total length the length of the fish from the mouth to the tail compressed to its fullest length

tributary a stream that feeds into another stream, river or lake

turbid cloudy; water clouded by suspended sediments or plant matter that limits visibility and the passage of light

velocity the speed of water flowing in a stream or river

vent the opening at the end of the digestive tract

ventral the underside of the fish

vertebrate an animal with a backbone

vomerine teeth teeth on the roof of the mouth

warmwater a non-salmonid species of fish that lives in water that routinely exceeds 70 degrees F; also used to describe a lake or river according to average summer temperature

yolk the part of an egg containing food for the developing fish

zooplankton the animal component of plankton; tiny animals that float or swim weakly; common food of fry and small fish

REFERENCES

Much of the information for this book came from research presentations, the U.S. Fish and Wildlife Service, U.S. Geological Survey and state, provincial and university departments of conservation, fisheries and wildlife—most notably the Arizona Game and Fish Department's Heritage Data Management System. Other valuable sources of information include the titles listed below:

Bosanko, David. 2007
Fish of Minnesota Field Guide
Adventure Publications, Inc.

Hanophy, Wendy. 2006
Native Fish of Colorado's Eastern Plains
Colorado Division of Wildlife

Johnson, Dan. 2007
Fish of Colorado Field Guide
Adventure Publications, Inc.

Minckley, W.L. 1973
Fishes of Arizona
Arizona Game and Fish Department

Pflieger, William. 1997
Fishes of Missouri, The
Missouri Department of Conservation

Sternberg, Dick. 1987
Freshwater Gamefish of North America
Cy DeCosse, Inc.

INDEX

ABOUT THE AUTHOR

Dan Johnson is an author and lifelong student of freshwater fish and fishing. For nearly two decades he has brought North American anglers breaking news on the latest scientific research, fishing techniques and related technology. Dan is a longtime attendee of American Fisheries Society annual conferences and related symposia. He is a syndicated weekly newspaper columnist, and has published more than 200 feature articles nationwide in the pages of *North American Fisherman*, *Walleye In-Sider* and other publications. Dan has also made numerous fishing-related TV appearances on ESPN2, and is the author of *Fish of Colorado Field Guide*. Above all, he is a passionate angler who enjoys spending time on the water with his family, patterning fish behavior and observing how these fascinating creations interact with one another in the underwater web of life. He resides in Cambridge, Minnesota, with wife, Julie, and children, Emily, Jacob and Joshua.